SABRINA FISHER REECE

UNBROKEN

Mending the Holes Left by Life

Contents

Preface

This book was not written from a place of having it all figured out. It was written from the quiet, sacred space that comes after survival, when the noise settles just enough for truth to surface. It was written by someone who learned early how to endure, how to adapt, and how to keep going even when the heart was tired of being strong.

There were moments in my life when sadness felt like a permanent residence rather than a passing visitor. Moments when the weight of memory made it difficult to breathe fully, let alone hope freely. Trauma has a way of creating invisible fractures inside us, small at first, then deeper with every unprocessed loss, every unanswered question, every moment we were forced to grow up too fast. Over time, those fractures can begin to feel like holes, places where safety, trust, or joy once lived.

For a long time, I believed those holes meant I was broken beyond repair. I believed that what had happened to me defined me, that the sadness I carried was evidence of weakness rather than survival. Depression and fear did not arrive as strangers; they settled in quietly, convincing me that this heaviness was simply who I was now.

But this book exists because that was not the end of the my story. Healing did not come all at once. It did not arrive neatly or dramatically. It came in fragments. In moments of reflection. In learning how to sit with myself without running. In recognizing that pain does not erase love, and suffering does not cancel purpose. Slowly, I began to understand that the holes left by life were not proof of my destruction, but invitations to mend with intention.

This book is about that mending those holes left behind by life. It is about learning how to tend to your inner world with the same care you once used to survive it. It is about acknowledging what hurt without letting it become your identity. It is about understanding that even after deep trauma, the heart is capable of repair, not by becoming harder, but by becoming more honest, more compassionate, and more grounded in truth.

If you are holding this book, there is a reason. Perhaps you recognize yourself in the quiet exhaustion of carrying too much for too long. Maybe you have learned how to function, but not how to feel safe inside your own body or mind. Perhaps you sense that healing is possible, but you are unsure where to begin.

This book does not promise to erase the past. It offers something far more meaningful. A path back to yourself. A reminder that you are not defined by what you endured, but by what you choose to mend. A gentle reassurance that even with scars, even with holes, you are still whole.

You are not alone, you are not beyond healing.

One

Our Holes

Unfortunately, this world is filled with hurt people. People who have endured pain, death, loss, tragedy, abandonment, and disappointments of every imaginable kind. For a long time, I truly believed I was alone in my despair. I thought my experiences were rare, that what I had lived through was too extreme, too dark, too complicated for anyone else to understand. Because of that belief, I stayed silent. I kept my story tucked away, convinced that if people knew where I came from, they would see me differently.

Shame has a way of isolating us, even when we are surrounded by others. Because I was unwanted and rejected by my mother, I subconsciously believed rejection was inevitable everywhere else in my life. I assumed the world would treat me the same way she did. As a result, I walked through life with my defenses fully raised. Those defenses often showed up as attitude, impatience, and anger. To many people, I fit neatly into the stereotype of the angry woman. I accepted that label without protest because it created distance. Distance felt like safety. If people stayed away, they could not hurt me. If I did not bond deeply, I would not have to grieve another loss.

At the time, I had no idea how many hurt people were quietly walking around the world just like me. Those people believed as I did, that there was no fixing them ,and they would suffer from what they had been through forever.

It took years before I understood that my story was not unique in its pain, only in its details. Once I began opening up, I discovered how many people carried experiences eerily similar to mine. I met many other abandoned children who had grown into guarded adults. I met people living with un-diagnosed post-traumatic stress, depression, and anxiety who had never been given language for what they were experiencing. Before that realization, I rarely spoke about my past. I believed my trauma made me less than, unstable, or broken. I assumed that if people knew, they would treat me differently or pity me.

I also did not understand how directly my anger and depression were connected to what I had lived through. I did not recognize patterns or triggers. Nor did I know that emotional responses are often rooted in unhealed wounds. Instead, I thought something was fundamentally wrong with me. I labeled myself as crazy and worked hard to hide that version of myself from the world.

Opening up changed everything. When I finally allowed myself to speak honestly, I realized just how many people are surviving rather than living. There are countless individuals carrying pain they have never dealt with, wounds they have never examined, and trauma they have never been taught how to heal. Many are doing their best to function, show up, and appear strong, all while never seeking help or even realizing help exists.

That realization is one of the reasons sharing the tools that helped me is so important to me. I did not begin actively addressing my emotional and mental health until my late thirties. Looking back, I often wonder how different my life could have been if I had been given the language, awareness, and support earlier. My hope is that by sharing my journey and the tools that guided my healing, someone else will not have to wait as long as I did. Healing sooner changes everything.

Through my own reflection, I began to understand emotional wounds in a new way. I describe them as holes. These holes are formed by unresolved pain, trauma, abandonment, and loss that were never properly addressed. They are not visible, but they are deeply felt.

For many years, I walked around with massive holes in my heart. As time passed and I became more aware, I started to see those same holes reflected in the lives of others. Some people's holes were even larger than mine. If left unattended, these holes do not remain small. They expand in a dangerous way. Life continues moving forward, and we often move with it, unaware that we are bleeding emotionally into our relationships, our decisions, and our sense of self.

These unhealed wounds do not just affect us. They affect everyone we love. They interfere with our ability to give and receive love the way God intended for us to. We were created to love naturally and without fear, but when love is denied early in life, fear becomes our teacher instead. The heart adapts by protecting itself, even if that protection causes harm later.

I came to believe that small pieces of our soul escape through these holes. We spend much of our lives trying to retrieve those small lost pieces and put ourselves back together again, attempting to feel like a whole again. Unfortunately, in that process, we often hurt others, sometimes without even realizing it. There were moments when I genuinely did not understand why my reactions were so intense or explosive. My friends and family did not understand either. To them, I was simply hot-headed.

One example stands out clearly.

Years ago, my ex-husband made an innocent comment while we were walking through the mall. He mentioned liking a particular pair of shoes a woman was wearing. There was no ill intent behind his words. He meant no harm whatsoever. In a healthy emotional state, it would have meant nothing. I probably would have even agreed that the shoes were nice. But because my holes were still open and unhealed, my mind translated his comment into something entirely different. I heard, "She is better than you." I heard, "You are not enough."

What followed was not rational. It was reactive. I went home, gathered every pair of shoes I owned, and threw them at him in a rage, shouting accusations that had nothing to do with him and everything to do with my unresolved wounds. Today, we can laugh about it. At the time, it was painful, confusing, and damaging.

The truth was simple but devastating. Because my mother did not love me, I was terrified that no one ever truly would. Even when love was present, I did not trust it. Until I learned to love myself and began closing my holes, I could not fully accept love from anyone else.

As I began doing the work, everything shifted. Growth started with identifying my triggers and understanding why they existed. That required digging into my past and connecting painful dots I had avoided for years. The process was uncomfortable, but it gave me clarity. With clarity came freedom.

Another moment that revealed the depth of my wounds happened when I was eighteen. My older sister had left for college, and I was living with my aunt Sabra. When my sister told me she would not be coming home for the holidays, I fell apart. Her decision was normal, reasonable, and had nothing to do with me, but my heart could not process it that way. All I felt was abandonment all over again.

I reacted from fear, not reality At that point in my life, loss felt constant. My father, who loved me had died when I was ten. My mother was absent and still dealing with the drug addiction that prevented her from raising me. My world felt unstable, and my emotional responses reflected that instability.

It would take years before I understood that my behavior was rooted in feeling unworthy. Nothing truly changes until we acknowledge our wounds and choose to heal them. Physical wounds heal naturally, but emotional wounds require intention. Whatever method helps you begin closing your "Holes," I urge you to pursue it. Healing brings peace that once felt impossible.

Forgiveness was a crucial part of my healing. Forgiving my mother allowed a hole I had lived with for decades to finally begin closing.

So I ask you now, gently and honestly, what is the source of your holes? What pain are you still carrying? Take time to reflect. Identify the experiences that shaped them. Consider who you may need to forgive, or who you may need to ask forgiveness from. This book is for your growth. Be honest with yourself. That honesty can change the course of your life.

In order to live a better quality of life, we must stop allowing the past to hold us hostage. We must accept what was and choose to move toward healing.

Happiness is not a fantasy. It becomes unreachable only when we refuse to face what hurt us.

Let us raise children who will not have to recover from their past.

Healing does not require you to rush or force answers before you are ready. It asks only that you become willing to look inward with compassion instead of judgment. The holes you carry are not proof of weakness; they are evidence that you survived something that required you to adapt. When you acknowledge them without shame, you begin the process of mending them. Each moment of awareness, each choice to respond with intention instead of fear, gently stitches together the places where life once tore you open.

This book is not here to reopen your wounds, but to walk with you as you learn how to heal them. You are not broken, and you never were. What you experienced shaped you, but it does not define you. As you move forward, remember that healing is not about erasing the past. It is about reclaiming your power in the present and choosing to live with clarity, courage, and self-love. The journey begins here, not because everything is fixed, but because you are finally ready to mend what life could not destroy.

Two

Tragedies of Life

Many horrible things have happened to so many people throughout their lives. A huge amount of us have endured trauma, abuse, death and disappointment. Some incidents have been so horrendous we do not feel we can ever move forward in life.

When I was seventeen years old, less than thirty days away from my high school graduation, I personally witnessed a tragedy that changed my life forever.

My grandfather, grandmother, her youngest son who was my father, my sister and I lived in a large home in Compton on 126th st. It had three gigantic bedrooms, a full size kitchen and service porch. There was a large separate living room and dining room, a long hallway, two bathrooms, and a massive backyard with a huge avocado tree. The property had another smaller home in the back that my father's sister SaBra (who I was named after) lived.

We were happy, healthy children, very well taken care of by our grandmother. My grandparents were both born in Dallas, Texas and were poor growing up as children, so they were determined to make sure they never experienced lack once they moved to California. We always had more than enough food. There was a large, deep freezer in our home that they kept stocked with food. We were not rich but we weren't poor either.

Quite often my grandmother would tell us stories of her childhood in Texas. She would tell us that she could take a quarter and buy and loaf of bread and a slab of salami. She told us so many stories of having only one pair of shoes and having to walk from North Dallas to South Dallas to school everyday. Looking back, I wish I would have paid more attention to those priceless stories.

It this day and age we would of had cell phone cameras to take pictures and videos of our ancestors. It would be amazing to have footage of my grandmother, but all my memories are inside of me.

My grandmother my older sister Mary and myself in the front yard of our home on 126th st in Compton

My grandfather and grandmother did not have any children together. They met in Dallas after my grandmothers divorce from her first husband Charlie Fisher.

My sister and I were the only two children of her youngest son, so when our mother couldn't take care of us due to her drug addiction, my grandmother gladly took over. My sister and I were infants, only 11 and 3 months old when she took us into her home. She was sixty-nine years old and had already raised three children of her own. I'm sure the decision to take on children that small, that most likely were born with drugs in their systems could not have been an easy one, but she did it wholeheartedly and willingly.

My grandfather was not the biological father of my grandmother's three children. He was her second husband who had moved her and her children to California from Dallas to give them a better life.

My grandmother didn't speak a lot about their relationship when we were children, but it was always clear to us even as small kids that he was not the love of her life. He was simply a nice man who was a great provider who moved her and her children from Dallas to California in the 1950's. I never knew my grandmother to work her husband was the sole provider in our household.

Although our grandfather lived in the home with us for the entire seventeen years my sister and I were there, I don't remember having a lot of personal interaction with him. I have no memory of any parental advice at all. I can clearly remember my father and my grandmother taking time to talk to and teach us things as we grew up but I don't ever remember my grandfather talking to us or telling us stories. In retrospect I find that unusual but it was just normal to us back then. I also don't recall having a need or urge to bond with him either.

He cut grass for a living so there were always large lawn mowers in our home. The only outfit I ever remember him wearing was a pair of green overalls. His legal name was McClendon Fair but we all called him Mack.

He was a tall man, at least 6 foot 3 inches. I can't say for sure if he was soft spoken, I can only say that I don't have any real memory of what his voice sounded like. He spoke to us so rarely. He definitely never yelled at us or my grandmother. I don't even remember ever hearing them argue.

My last year of high school, I was alone in my room when my grandmother came into my room with a concerned look on her face. I was laying on my bed and she stood there with her hands on her hips with a worried look. She said, *"Mack said he was gonna kill me."* She seemed worried but, like I said I had never witnessed him abuse or even raise his voice at her our entire childhood.

Being raised in the church, I was taught that prayer fixes everything. I responded and said to her *"Well Mama, if you know where he keeps the gun then please go take it and remove the bullets."* Once she left my room I got onto my knees and prayed, *"God, Mama doesn't seem happy. I love her, please make her happy."*

The next day was Sunday, May 3, 1997. I was only 17 years old but I was in a committed relationship with a young man who would later become my first husband. He worked as a security guard and was coming to pick me up one day after his shift. I was aimlessly walking through the house from room to room to pass the time until he arrived.

I went into my grandparents room which was a very large bedroom that had been added onto the home. It was the size of a large living room. I walked into their room and immediately noticed a gun laying on the television stand. I instantly reflected back to the conversation my grandmother and I had the day before when I had told her to remove the bullets from the gun. I walked over to the gun and picked it up. Only because of my boyfriend's profession and the fact that he carried a 357 magnum himself which he had recently demonstrated the workings of did I know how check the gun to see if my grandmother had indeed removed the bullets like I suggested to her the day before.

I picked up the gun, opened the cylinder, noticed that the bullets were still in the gun. I slowly started to turn the gun downward and allow the six bullets to slide out of the cylinder and into the palm of my hand. Instantly I thought, *"SaBrina you are being silly, they have been married for thirty-two years"* So I

9

stopped just as the bullets were half way out and i turned the gun upward and let the bullets slide back into the gun. The gun was so old and rusty I was afraid to pop the cylinder closed.

My grandmother and grandfather were both in the kitchen. I walked onto the service porch, which is next to the kitchen, and said to my grandfather as I held the gun with the open cylinder in my left hand. I said *"I opened your gun, but I'm afraid to close it."* He was sitting in his normal seat at the kitchen table and my grandmother was standing directly across from him. He looked up at me and responded, *"What are you doing with my gun? Do not play with guns!"* I replied, *"Clyde taught me how to open it."* Clyde was my current boyfriend.

My grandfather got up from the table and took the gun out of my hand and sat back down at the table. He sat the gun on the kitchen table and continued to lecture me about gun safety.

Instantly, my grandmother who was still standing picked up the gun and immediately turned it away from both of us pointing in the direction of a window that was behind her. She began to refer to the weight of the gun, she bounced it up and down saying *"This gun is heavy, Verie (who was a relative of hers) has a gun like this."* As soon as her hand came down from the bouncing, the gun went off behind her under the window. The startling sound caused me to run, but I heard my grandfather say to her, *"You tried to kill me."* I could hear his kitchen chair scraping the floor as he pushed back. I stopped and immediately returned to the doorway of the kitchen in time to see my grandfather remove the gun from my grandmother's hand and shoot her in the head.

Things appeared to be moving in slow motion. It seemed as though I saw the hole begin to form in my grandmothers head. I saw her body slowly begin to slump and fall to the ground. I believed I would be next, so I turned and ran through the house and out the front door. I kept running until I got six doors down to a neighbor's home. This was the house of childhood friends we had grown up with, Reuben, Lavonne and Craig (who would later become KAM, the famous rapper from Compton).

I ran up to the door and began to beat on the door hysterically. Someone opened the door and I began to scream, *"My grandfather killed my grand-*

mother!"

I'm not sure if I blacked out after that, but when I returned outside from their house the streets were blocked and there were loud sirens, it seemed like utter chaos. My entire world changed that day. Life as I knew it would never be the same.

I have carried the memory of that tragic day with me for years. I have replayed that memory over and over in my head for what felt like a lifetime. I re-traumatized myself with the visual images of my grandmothers lifeless body falling to the floor after being shot in the head by my grandfather, her husband of 32 years.

Although this happened when I was a child, I held this horrible memory in my mind for years and I suffered from it well into my late 40s. I had nightmares of that day for decades. The scene of her death played like a movie in my mind repeatedly. I had come to terms with the fact that I would forever be plagued with this memory and the pain of this devastating day.

I have since learned that despite the tragedy of the incident, my lifelong suffering from it is still a choice. This can be a hard concept for people to grasp. No one wants to believe that they had anything to do with their own continued suffering.

Suffering is a choice.

What I witnessed was traumatic and no child should ever have to see the slaughter of anyone let alone a loved one. After years of replaying the day in my head, I have come to realize that that day has long passed and I do not have to revisit it. Doing so has caused years of suffering which negatively affected my mental and physical well being. I had no idea I could choose to stop replaying that horror movie in my head. Once I learned to press "stop" instead of "play" my suffering began to subside.

Just because we experience pain does not mean we have to endure that pain for the rest of our lives. We must learn the tools to eject those negative thoughts and images that cause us so much pain. Continuing to suffer from past trauma is a conscious choice. We must make peace with our past and eventually turn the movie off. It can be hard for people to accept that we choose to replay the past.

"Past trauma creates changes in our lives that we don't get to choose. Healing is about creating change that we <u>can</u> choose."

We are doing a disservice to ourselves by not allowing ourselves to move forward emotionally. Staying stuck in the pain of the past can be a detriment to our lives. We must cast out these memories and make a conscious choice not to relive them.

Visualize past traumatic memories like a speeding tennis ball headed straight toward you, but now you have the racquet and the ability to not let the tennis ball hit you as it has so many times in the past. Stand strong and swat the tennis ball away aggressively, hit the ball so hard it flies up and over into the atmosphere, so far away that it disappears and never returns.

I have another visualization technique that helps me feel safe when I am driving. I used to drive a very large truck, a hummer H2, for ten years and I always felt safe. When I changed to a much smaller car that was lower to the ground I found myself experiencing a lot of anxiety whenever I would drive. I was fearful that I would get into an accident and because the car was so small I would not survive it. I know the danger of allowing fearful thoughts to persist in your mind, so I created a visual of my little silver car wrapped in a protective bubble. I convinced myself that this bubble was impenetrable and that it would protect me and my children as we rode in the vehicle.

The mind is such a powerful tool. More powerful that we can even imagine. Whatever we train our mind to believe becomes reality.

"It is done unto you as you believe."
-Matthew 9:29-

Tragedy changes us whether we are ready or not. When something violent, sudden, and irreversible enters your life, it does not simply become a memory.

It reshapes your nervous system, your beliefs about safety, and the way you move through the world. Witnessing the murder of my grandmother altered the way I understood love, loss, and permanence. For years, I lived as if danger could appear at any moment, as if peace was temporary and grief was permanent. That kind of trauma does not disappear just because time passes. It settles into the body and the mind, quietly influencing how we think, feel, and respond.

What I eventually learned is that while we cannot change what happened, we can change how it continues to live inside us. Healing did not come from pretending the tragedy never occurred or minimizing its impact. It came from acknowledging the pain honestly and refusing to let it define the rest of my life. The beliefs formed in trauma may feel real, but they are not always true. With intention, awareness, and patience, those beliefs can be softened and reshaped. This chapter is not about reliving loss, but about recognizing that even after unimaginable tragedy, it is possible to reclaim your inner world. The pain may be part of your story, but it does not get to write the ending.

Three

How Being Positive Changed My Life

There is absolutely nothing perfect about being positive. It's hard and requires focus and endurance. Positivity is a learned behavior and must become second nature to be maintained. This book will teach you practical skills on how to be and stay positive, no matter what's happening or what has happened in your life. Life unfolds for us all, and it's not always filled with happy, wonderful moments. We must learn how to navigate the harder times and not let them consume us mentally. While we cannot control everything that happens in the world around us, we can learn to control how we think, and how we react.

One thing I like to remind myself is that even though many negative situations actually exist in our lives in real time, more than half of them only exist in our minds. We often fear negative circumstances that never actually happen. We think hundreds of negative thoughts daily, not realizing the damage these thoughts alone can cause. We fear pain, sadness, failure, heartbreak, and more. Allowing those fears to occupy the majority of our mind space can prevent us from enjoying this amazing world.

First, we need to develop tools to immediately recognize negative thoughts and then stop ourselves from thinking them in order to eliminate the mental chaos. Next, we must learn to empower ourselves mentally and emotionally. We can take full control of our thinking patterns and replace all negative thoughts with positive ones. Negative thoughts are garbage that we must discard. They can't stay around because they will grow and take over your mind. Even if these thought are coming from real memories of things that actually happened to us, we still must avoid constantly allowing them space in our mind.

Negative thoughts are the internal enemy and we must treat them as such. You can't hang out with them, touch them, or look them in the face and converse with them. This enemy is unseen, but is the most important enemy of them all. Negative thoughts must go! They mean absolutely no good and must be eliminated.

Only you can rid yourself of a negative thinking pattern. No one can do it for you. This book provides ideas and tools, but you have to be committed to doing the actual work yourself. The work I speak of may be taxing at times, and you may want to give up, but please don't. The reward for changing a negative thinking pattern into a positive one is priceless. this is how you become "*Unbroken.*" Changing your mindset and learning how to maintain a positive state of mind will be one of the best decisions you ever make. That one decision alone will drastically improve your quality of life.

Once I realized I controlled the suffering that negative thoughts brought me, my quality of life changed for the better. Recognizing my power to eliminate negative thoughts allowed me to create a better life for myself where I didn't have to remind myself of every perceived flaw. I don't have to relive my past trauma, and neither do you.

Past trauma is just that, past. It's not happening to you now. I know so many of you have experienced terrible things in your life, just like me. I am so sorry that you had to endure those things. I love you and I pray you seek, find and sustain healing. But you don't have to keep suffering by bringing it back to life in your mind. Stop the self-torment and realize that you have been the tormentor, choosing to continue negative thinking. You are the one driving the bus. Remind yourself of happier times in your life. I mean that in love, not taking away the seriousness of what you have been through at all. I just truly want you to find peace mentally and emotionally.

I'm not saying it is easy to let go of the horrible, painful experiences of the past. I have had my share of tragic events, too. The injustices you may have endured are valid. However, you do not have to suffer from the effects forever. No matter how hard it is to let it go, it is vital to do so if you want to live a wonderful life. You must release the anger and resentment that may still linger. Holding on to anger, hurt, and resentment doesn't hurt others; it hurts you.

I was an abandoned child and suffered many childhood traumas because of my mother's drug addiction. However, right now, in the present moment, I am not living through those situations, they are in my past. But every time I thought of them, I experienced their pain again. I would mentally relive the devastation of the events, causing myself the pain and hurt.

It's a difficult concept to teach others, but continuously thinking about past abuse, hurt, and pain is a choice. We can stop those thoughts. We can say, "Nope, not today," and push those thoughts right out of our heads. Yes, they will return, but we must be consistent. We can choose to focus only on positive thoughts. When negative thoughts come, acknowledge them first, because you cannot change what you are in denial about. We cannot heal what we hide. Acknowledge the negative emotions and thoughts, then cast them out and replace them with positive options.

Imagine memories as if they are videos. You don't have to keep replaying them or rewinding to watch again. Stop replaying negative memories and focus on moving forward in your life. It's the only way to a bright and happy future. Everyone deserves a happy and positive life, but first we must believe it is possible.

Many people ask me, "How do you stay so positive?" I don't wake up feeling positive every day. For example, if I wake up in a negative space, I immediately start using the tools I've learned to help me return to a positive headspace. I'll share the tools that work best for me, but you will need to find those that work best for your life. I firmly believe in having practical tools to maintain a positive state of mind. Try out a few different tools to see which fit well into your life. Choose tools and practices that you believe in wholeheartedly and are more likely to sustain.

To stay positive, I use the following tools:

1. Positive Affirmations

Speaking positive statements aloud to myself. For example:

- I am beautiful
- I am happy.
- I am successful.
- My business is a great success.
- I am worthy of love.
- I am in great health.
- My life is peaceful.
- Money flows easily and frequently into my life.

2. Creative Visualization

Learn to create a visual image in your head. Picture yourself in the new home you desire or sitting at the desk of that new job you feel you deserve. Visualize your magical wedding day to the partner who possesses all the qualities you desire. Close your eyes and create the images in your mind's eye. If it's a car you desire, see that car in your mind. Picture the specific details: the color of the exterior and interior, the seats, and dashboard color. Imagine yourself gratefully driving around, hands on the steering wheel. Remember, everything that exists was a picture in someone's mind first.

3. Meditation

Learning to be still is one of the best tools I have ever learned. Simply sitting in a quiet place and breathing. Most of us are too busy with the hustle and bustle of life to just sit still and focus on our breathing patterns. As simple as it seems, it's not. It requires focus and discipline. Our mind speaks to us all day, but we are too busy to hear it. Once we learn the art of being still, only then can we notice when we are having negative thoughts. In order to change negative thoughts into positive ones, we first have to notice they are there. You can't change something until you acknowledge its existence. Meditation allows you the quiet time needed to recognize the things you need to change.

4. Mirror Work

Mirror work is priceless and unbelievably effective. Just stand in front of a mirror and speak the affirmations you created aloud, as I suggested in #1. Look at yourself and say uplifting things repeatedly until you believe them. The DNA cells in your body can actually hear you, so be repetitive and consistent. Repeating powerful, encouraging words is like planting seeds in a garden. Eventually, they will grow, just like plants in a garden. The constant repetition is like water; without it, the things we plant die. Similarly, without reinforcing affirmations, our mind and body won't accept the new thoughts. We must repeat them until we truly believe them. This will allow us to generate the feelings needed to manifest them into our lives.

5. Reading

I write books because reading books changed my life. Reading stories of perseverance and determination showed me I do not have to identify as a victim for the rest of my life. I have survived a few tragedies, and books gave me hope that the pain would eventually cease. Reading allowed me to see different perspectives and taught me I didn't have to accept every thought as fact. It revealed my inner power and my ability to be happy despite early childhood traumas. The same applies to each of you. Reading helped me view the world differently and understand the importance of balance. Good and bad will always exist, but books helped me realize that light will eventually emerge from the darkness. I read every chance I get and will continue writing books for as long as I live. Books and the vast knowledge within them are essential to our mental and spiritual growth.

6. Grounding/Earthing

There is value in taking time to plant your feet directly in the soil. Walking on grass or untreated concrete grounds us and connects us with the natural properties of the Earth. It's something I didn't learn until my fifties, and I truly wish I had known about it earlier in life. We are so conditioned to covering our feet with shoes that the idea of going barefoot rarely occurs to us. Our amazing Mother Earth possesses powerful healing properties, and research has proven that going barefoot offers numerous health benefits. Planting our feet in the grass or on un-coated concrete can help our bodies heal from various ailments. Sometimes, conventional medicine doesn't seem to work, and we have nothing to lose by walking in nature. Why not? Many of us are wary of man-made medicine, which often has side effects. I'm not suggesting anyone stop taking their medication, but there is no harm in incorporating practices that allow you to reconnect with nature.

7. Stillness

"Be still and know that I am God" (Psalms 46:10). The older you get, the more you understand the importance of stillness. Simply shutting down the mouth and mind and sitting quietly gives you a chance to observe and process the present moment. As I age, this practice becomes increasingly valuable to my life. Every morning, your body may not feel at its best, but taking a few minutes to sit in stillness and breathe will help ensure a better start to the day's journey.

Four

The Woman I Became After the Storm

I did not become who I am by accident. I became her by necessity. When I look back now, I can see how early life forced me into decisions that most people my age were never asked to make. At nineteen years old, I got married, not because I had some grand romantic vision of marriage, but because I did not have anywhere else to go. My grandmother, the woman who raised me, had just been murdered. My mother was still lost in addiction and chaos. The foundation of my life had collapsed, and I was standing in the rubble trying to survive.

So I married my boyfriend. I was nineteen. He was older, in his early twenties. At that age, marriage felt like safety. It felt like structure. It was the closest thing to stability I could reach for in the middle of so much loss. Looking back, I understand that I was not choosing a husband as much as I was choosing shelter from the storm.

We went on to build a life, imperfect as it was. We had a son, Justin. Becoming a mother changed me in ways I did not yet have language for. I was still a child myself in many ways, still grieving, still carrying unprocessed trauma, but I knew one thing with absolute certainty. I was going to protect my child. I was going to love him. He would never feel unwanted like I was made to feel by my mother. I was going to do better than what had been done to me, and I did just that.

Years later, I had another child, my daughter Joi. By then, the cracks in my marriage had widened into something dangerous. My husband had become abusive. He hit women, and even though I was young, even though I had no real money, no formal education, and no clear plan, I found the courage to leave. That decision still matters to me. I am proud of that woman. Many women my age would have stayed, not because they wanted to, but because they felt trapped. I was terrified, but I knew I could not raise my children in violence. I knew that staying would cost me something I might never get back.

I left with what I had, and never looked back. What I did have was my hands. I knew how to braid hair. That skill became my lifeline.

In April of 1996, on the corner of 65th and Normandie, I gave birth to *Braids By SaBrina*. I did not have investors. I did not have a business plan typed up neatly in a folder. What I had was determination, intuition, and a God-given ability to see opportunity where others saw limitation. I walked the neighborhood advertising my services.I put fliers advertising the new braiding shop that was coming. I bought tables and chairs from target. I talked to people. I learned quickly that marketing is not always about money. Sometimes it is about courage, consistency, and connection.

I was raising two children. Justin was six years old. Joi was just a year old. I was scared. I was still carrying enormous pain from my past. But every day, I showed up anyway. Braiding hair was not just work for me. It was how I survived with dignity. It was a way to stand on my own feet when everything else in my life had once been taken from me.

That small beginning grew into something much larger than I ever imagined.

I later moved the business to Adams Boulevard, where it would live for three decades. For thirty years, *Braids By SaBrina* was more than a salon. It became a household name. It was a community hub. I employed women who needed a chance. I taught them skills, not just in hair, but in life. I taught them how to save money. I taught them how to believe in themselves. I taught them that entrepreneurship was not reserved for people with privilege. It was available to those willing to work, learn, and persist.

All of this happened while I was still healing. My spiritual journey did not begin because life was easy. It began because pain demanded answers. I needed to understand why my mother abandoned me. I needed to understand how a woman could put her three-month-old baby into a suitcase during a drug binge and attempt to end her life. That truth took years to face without breaking. My grandmother saved me and took me and raised me. She loved me wholeheartedly. she was a loving kind, christian woman with old schools moral and values, that she instilled in me. Then she was taken from me violently.

No one should have to heal from witnessing something so horrible at a young age. That kind of loss does not simply disappear with time. It settles into the body. It shows up in reactions, relationships, and quiet moments when no one else is watching.

Yet I kept building. I received recognition from the City Council. I was featured in the *Wave* newspaper, the *Sentinel*, the *LA Watts Times*, the *Sacramento Observer*, the *Final Call* and eventually the *Wall Street Journal*. I became instrumental in helping change laws in California, allowing natural hair care professionals to operate without being forced through cosmetology licensing that did not reflect our craft. That work mattered. It was advocacy born from lived experience. I contributed to and lead others in the community and still, I carried a lot of pain.

As the years went by, something shifted. I began to tell my story. I started speaking on stages at, churches, schools, women empowerment events etc. At first, it was raw and overwhelming. I cried on stage. I cried talking about my grandmother's murder. I cried acknowledging that I was an unwanted child. Each time I spoke, it took something out of me emotionally. But I noticed something important. People were listening, and more than that, people were seeing themselves in my story.

That realization changed the direction of my life. I understood that my survival was not just for me. It was meant to be shared.

I became a motivational speaker. I spoke on more than forty-eight stages throughout Los Angeles and surrounding communities. I was flown to Louisiana by a group of accomplished Black businesswomen to speak. I invested in myself. I hired speech trainers, Dr. Will Moreland and Dr. Delatorro McNeal II, because I knew that having a testimony was not enough. I had a responsibility to tell it with clarity, purpose, and care.

Slowly, something else happened. I stopped crying when I told the story. Not because it no longer mattered, but because it no longer owned me.

Now, at fifty-six years old, I can say this with confidence. I am proud of the woman I became after the storm. I have employed over 1700 women women. I have been blessed to have had the opportunity to mentor them. I have watched them grow into business owners themselves. I have helped change laws. I have raised children. I have turned pain into purpose without pretending the pain never existed.

And now, I am building again. With *In 59 Seconds Publishing Company*, I am teaching others that their stories matter. That their voices deserve to be preserved. That writing a book does not have to take five years of fear and self-doubt. You literary legacy matters and will leave a impact on the lives of others for generations to come. Stories heal generations.

The woman I became did not arrive overnight. She was built one hard decision at a time. If my story proves anything, it is this. You can come from unimaginable loss and still create something meaningful. You can carry pain and still contribute beauty to the world. You can be unbroken.

'Straight Outta Compton'

Braids by SaBrina

The Sacramento Observer

SIX-TIME WINNER OF THE JOHN B. RUSSWURM TROPHY FOR JOURNALISM EXCELLENCE

MARCH 18 - 24, 1999   The Observer Newspapers   PAGE B-3

Braiders March To Support Bill

Licensing Not Fair, Salon Owners Say

by STEENA STEWARD
OBSERVER Staff Writer

Sandra Faber-Reese, a Los Angeles hair braider whose salon was raided in 1996, expresses her concerns.

OBSERVER Photo by ROBERT MARYLAND

Helen Hatchett, owner of K.I.N.K.S. International. They have left her hair braiding to stylists from the Bay Area and Los Angeles during a march to the State Capitol to support a bill that would extend hair braiders from having to get a cosmetology license.

Smith-Dee Uqdah, president of the American Hair Braiders and Natural Hair braiders association, came from Washington D.C. to Sacramento to support AB 133.

Assemblywoman Elaine Minghet of San Francisco, author of Bill AB 133, feels that the administration of former Governor Pete Wilson, was very hard on the home operators and small businesses.

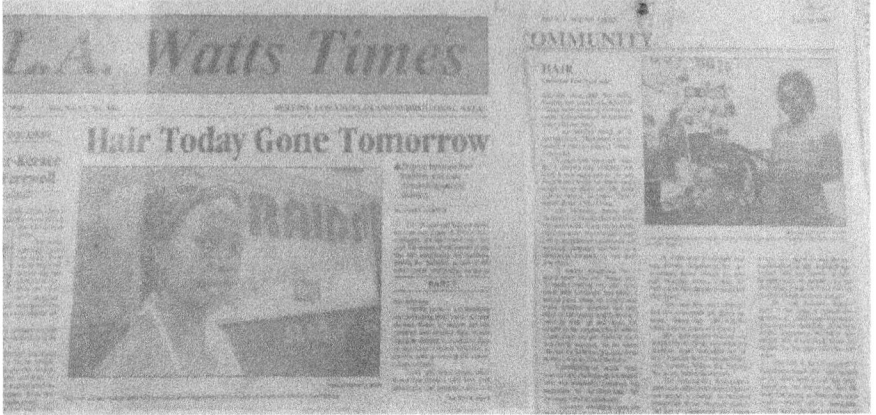

City of Compton
Resolution

COMPTON

Presented To

SaBrina Fisher Reece
In Honor of Your **15 Years of Service**

WHEREAS, in 1992 SaBrina Fisher Reece due to a community tragedy capitalized from her promotional signs being seen on local news channels, which lead to her phone constantly ringing with new business;

* * *

WHEREAS, In 1996 SaBrina Fisher Reece opened her 1st shop on 65th and Normandie;

* * *

WHEREAS, SaBrina Fisher Reece shortly after moved her business to La Brea and Adams Blvd;

* * *

WHEREAS, in 1998 SaBrina Fisher Reece and Braids by SaBrina was the target of an undercover sting by the California State Board of Cosmetology in order to govern braids salons in the same manner that barbershops and beauty salons were and abide by the same requirements. After 2 years of court battles SaBrina along with American Hairbraiders & Natural Hair Care Association and support of then Republican State Senator Ray Haynes fought off legislation requiring that hair braiders become licensed as cosmetologist, a story that eventually wound up in the Wall Street Journal;

* * *

WHEREAS, SaBrina Fisher Reece has serviced over 10,000 clients and has expanded her services to include twists, loc extensions, braid weaves and loc maintenance;

WHEREAS, SaBrina Fisher Reece over the last 15 years has hired 916 women and also speaks to inner-city youth and young women as a motivational speaker. She continues to teach others how to braid through the educational component of her business, which since 1998 has taught 360 students how to braid hair properly;

* * *

NOW, THEREFORE, be it resolved that I, Mayor Eric J. Perrodin, on behalf of the City of Compton and City Council Members, in recognition of your 15 years of dedicated service to the City of Los Angeles do hereby adjourn this 16th day of April 2011 honoring Ms. **SaBrina Fisher Reece**.

Eric J. Perrodin
Mayor

Barbara J. Calhoun
Council Member – District 1

Yvonne Arceneaux
Council Member – District 3

Lillie Dobson
Council Member – District 2

COMPTON

Dr. Willie O. Jones
Council Member – District 4

WALL STREET JOURNAL

SPETEMBER 4TH 1998

Get Out of Her Hair

SaBrina Reese is a 26-year-old entrepreneur who owns two African hair-braiding salons. In July, the state of California mounted an elaborate sting operation and cited her for not having a cosmetology license. Ms. Reese says the law requiring that hair-braiders have such a license is a relic of the "Jim Crow" era and she is fighting it in court.

Ms. Reese began braiding hair in high school and at-tually went to cosmetology school for a while. But braiding was neither included in the curriculum nor tested in the licensing exam, so she decided the 1,600 hours and $9,000 the school required were useless to her. Because her shops only braid hair and don't use chemi- and she now has nine employees.

Then last year, she was fined more than $1,000 by the state cosmetology board. She appealed the fine and had it reduced to $560. Last month, a state investigator pretending to be a customer entered her store and cited her and her employees for practicing "cosmetology" without a license. Ms. Reese faces a possible one-year jail sentence, but city prosecutors have declined to pursue the case for now, pending the outcome of a similar case in San Diego set to go to trial. Ms. Reese hopes the law being used against her will be thrown out as a result of a federal civil rights suit brought by the Institute for Justice. One of the plaintiffs is JoAnne Cornwell, a professor at San Diego State University, who says the anti-hair-braiding law "stifles the entrepreneurial urge in the community." The entrepreneurial urge is indeed common to the human spirit, and we don't

SABRINA —
CONGRATULATIONS
HOPE ALL IS WELL
John East___

Wave

Southwest Wave
Southwest Topics
Angeles Mesa & Tribune

THE COMMUNITIES OF CRENSHAW, BALDWIN HILLS, AND SOUTH LOS ANGELES

Vol. 80 No. 56 • Wednesday, August 12, 1998 • Copyright 1998, Wave Community Newspapers • 25¢

African Hairbraiding Now an Economic Civil Rights Issue

By NOVA BUNN
Staff Writer

LOS ANGELES — This is a story about money, race, politics, control and power — all in that order.

SaBrina Fibori Reese is a young woman divorced and responsible for the lives of two children who found a way to escape the welfare rolls by starting her African hairbraiding business. What was a legitimate business six years ago.

Like many African-American woman skilled in the craft of braiding, locking and braiding hair, Reese created hairstyles in her home for friends at a low rate, charging them only $20.

Today, Reese, 26, can command more than $250 per person to sit for nearly three hours in her large hair-braiding shops yield seven times the $ 4 million annually.

But, even after putting a business license and paying the required taxes, the state's Barbering and Cosmetology Program, formerly known as the California State Licensing Board of Barbering and Cosmetology, is trying to shut down Reese's hair salon for not complying with its regulations.

Ask what's because Reese and many other African hairbraiders say these regulations do not apply to their business.

"It's not right that they are trying to do to me," said Reese who now owns two hairbraiding shops and employs nine braiders.

"They want me to go to cosmetology school for something they don't teach and for classes I don't need because I don't work with chemicals.

The cosmetology program is arguing that hairbraiders, working in salons or out of their homes, fall under cosmetology certainty and should fulfill a required 1,600-hour course of study.

But most of those salaries, Reese said, have little to do with hair braiding.

African hairbraiding is a natural way of styling black hair that, without any chemicals, includes locking and twisting and oftentimes weaving extensions.

It's a skill many African-American women have learned at the knees of their mothers and grandmothers.

Last October, Reese was fined $1,000 by state regulators for not having a cosmetology license to practice Reese by her home.

After a court appearance, all but $560 was waived by the court.

In the latter case with no state, Reese believes the release of a lobby sting operation by the cosmetology program, in which an undercover

Continued on page 8

Photo from the LA Wave newspaper

SaBrina Reese, owner of two Braids by SaBrina salons, braids the hair of first-time customer Tertia Slacken.

African Hairbraiding Now an Economic Civil Rights Issue

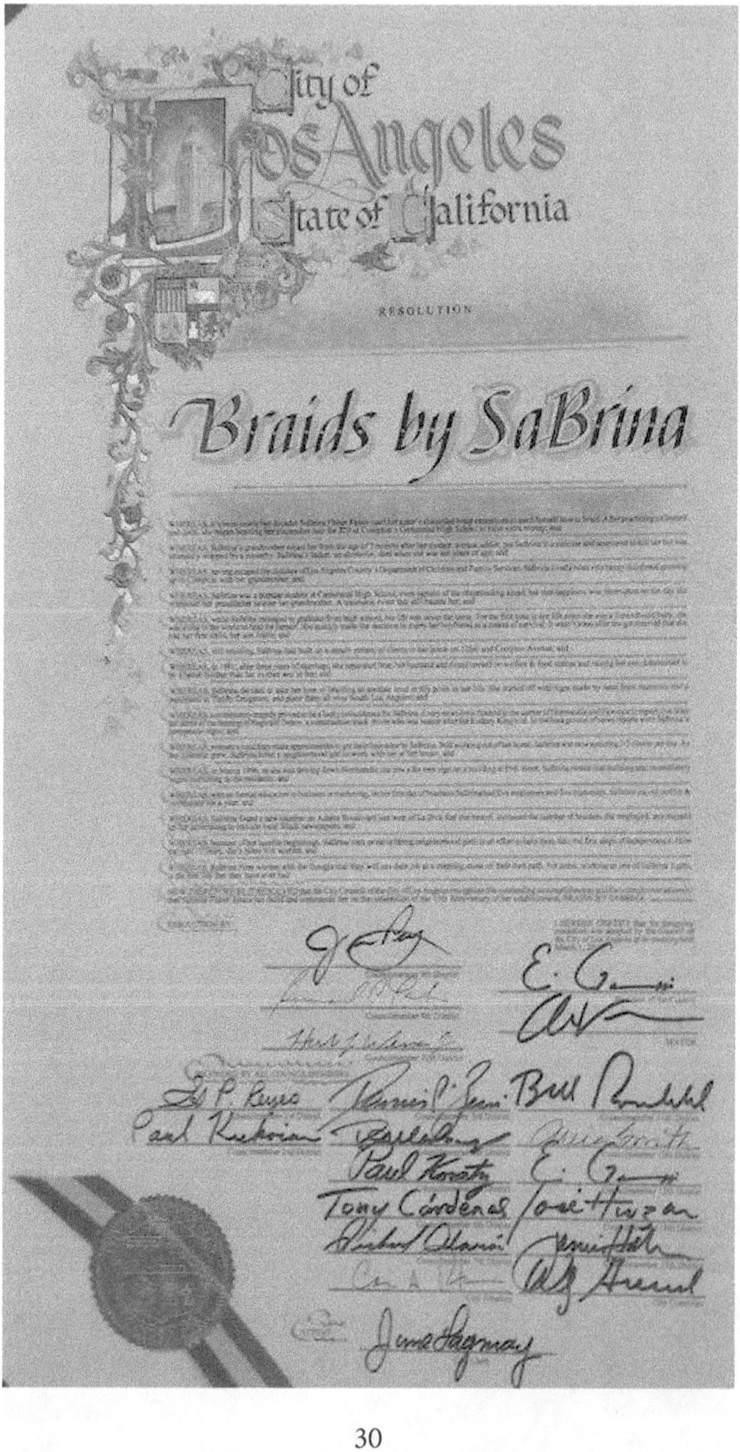

City of Los Angeles
State of California

RESOLUTION

Braids by SaBrina

When I joined Toastmaster to learn how to speak properly

Speaking to children at my daughters school

Speaking at Long Beach Job corps Graduation Ceremony

Five

What Didn't Break Me Taught Me

There was a time when I believed that everything I had been through was evidence that something was wrong with me. I looked at my life and saw a pattern of loss, abandonment, and pain, and I assumed it meant I was defective in some way. I could not yet see that the very things I thought disqualified me were quietly shaping me into someone with depth, discernment, and strength. I did not know then what I know now. What didn't break me was teaching me.

When you are living through trauma, it rarely feels instructional. It feels overwhelming and unfair. It feels like you are being asked to carry more than your share. When trauma happens early in life, before you have the language or emotional tools to process it, you internalize it. You do not say, "This experience is harmful." You say, "This must be who I am." That belief can follow you for decades if it is never challenged.

I spent years trying to outrun my past instead of understanding it. I stayed busy. I worked unnecessarily hard. I accomplished many things. On the outside, my life looked productive and successful. On the inside, I was still that little girl trying to make sense of why love disappeared so easily and why safety felt temporary. I did not yet understand that unhealed pain does not go away just because you become functional. It waits. It shows up in your reactions, your relationships, your fears, and the way you talk to yourself when no one else is listening.

What didn't break me taught me how deeply experiences imprint the mind and body. Trauma is not only a memory. It is a nervous system response. It's the way your body braces before your mind even catches up. It becomes the reason you react strongly to things that seem small to others. This is why your heart closes quickly or your temper rises suddenly. Understanding that changed how I saw myself. I stopped calling myself dramatic or broken and started asking better questions. What happened to me. What did I learn from it. What am I still carrying that no longer belongs to me.

One of the most important lessons I learned is that survival skills are not the same as life skills. The behaviors that kept me safe in one season became the very things that limited me in another. Being guarded protected me when I was young, but it also made it difficult to trust later in life. Being hyper independent helped me survive instability, but it also made it hard to receive support. Anger gave me a sense of power when I felt powerless, but it also pushed people away when what I actually needed was connection.

None of those responses made me weak. They made me adaptive. But adaptation is not the end of the story. Growth requires reflection. Healing requires honesty.

What didn't break me taught me that pain does not automatically make you wiser. Pain only teaches when you are willing to look at it without judgment. Many people suffer and never grow because they never stop long enough to examine what their experiences are trying to show them. They stay in survival mode for so long that it becomes familiar, even when it is painful. I know that place well. It feels safer to stay alert than to risk being hurt again. But staying alert forever is exhausting.

I also learned that strength does not always look like pushing through. Sometimes strength looks like slowing down and taking a breath. Sometimes it looks like admitting you are tired. It can look like asking for help even when you have been the helper for everyone else. For years, I wore my resilience like armor. I was proud of how much I could handle. I did not realize that I was using strength to avoid vulnerability. What didn't break me eventually taught me that vulnerability is not weakness. It is honesty.

There were seasons in my life when I was angry at God. I questioned why certain things were allowed to happen. I questioned why his protection seemed inconsistent. I wanted to know why love felt conditional. Faith did not always come easily to me. It evolved and deepened as times went by. It became less about answers and more about trust. I learned that spirituality is not about bypassing pain. It is about learning how to sit with it without letting it harden you.

What didn't break me taught me the difference between being alive and feeling alive. For a long time, I was functioning but not flourishing. I was doing what needed to be done, not what nourished my soul. Healing required me to pay attention to my inner world. It required me to notice what drained me and what restored me. It required me to get honest about patterns I kept repeating and why.

One of the hardest lessons was realizing that I could not heal by pretending everything was fine. Positivity without truth is just another form of avoidance. I had to allow myself to feel grief without rushing it. I had to let sadness exist without labeling it as failure. I learned to give myself permission to be human. What didn't break me taught me that emotions are not enemies. They are messengers.

I also learned that forgiveness is not about excusing harm. It is about freeing yourself from carrying it. Forgiveness does not mean what happened was acceptable. It means you are choosing not to let it define you forever. That distinction matters. For a long time, I resisted forgiveness because I thought it meant minimizing my pain or justifying the bad behavior of others. What I learned instead is that forgiveness is a boundary. It is a way of saying, "This stops here."

What didn't break me taught me how deeply the mind influences the quality of our lives. Thoughts become core beliefs. Beliefs become behaviors. Behaviors shape outcomes. When you grow up with instability, the mind learns to expect loss. It scans for danger even in safe moments. Healing required me to become aware of my thought patterns and gently challenge them. I had to ask myself whether the stories I was telling myself were true, or whether they were echoes of old wounds.

This work is not glamorous. It is quiet. It happens in moments when no one is applauding you. It happens when you choose to pause instead of react. It can happen when you choose to respond with intention instead of habit. Over time, those small choices add up. They begin to mend the holes life created.

What didn't break me also taught me compassion. When you have walked through deep pain, you begin to recognize it in others. You hear it in their tone. You see it in their defenses. You sense it in their silence. Compassion does not mean tolerating harm, but it does mean understanding that people are often fighting battles you cannot see. That understanding softened me. It made me less reactive and more discerning.

I learned that boundaries are a form of self respect. Saying no is not rejection. It is clarity. Choosing yourself does not mean you do not love others. It means you are no longer abandoning yourself to keep the peace. What didn't break me taught me that peace at the cost of self betrayal is not peace at all.

As the years passed, I began to see my life differently. I stopped asking why certain things happened and started asking what they shaped in me. I saw how adversity strengthened my intuition. I saw how loss deepened my empathy. I noticed how hardship sharpened my ability to lead, to teach, and to hold space for others. None of that erases the pain. It gives it purpose.

This chapter is not about glorifying suffering. I do not believe pain is necessary for growth, but I do believe that when pain happens, it can either close you off to the world or it can teach you how to survive in it. What didn't break me taught me how to stay open without being naive. I learned how to protect my heart without shutting it down. It taught me how to love with wisdom instead of fear.

If you are reading this and thinking about your own story, I want you to know something important. You are not behind. Healing is not linear. Growth does not follow a particular schedule. The fact that you are reflecting means you are already moving forward. What didn't break you is still teaching you, even now.

There is nothing wrong with you for needing time to process and heal. There is nothing wrong with you for still feeling the impact of things that happened long ago. Healing is not about erasing the past. It is about integrating it and allowing what you have lived to inform you without imprisoning you.

Today, I no longer see myself as a victim who survived despite her past. I see myself as someone who learned from it. I carry my experiences with awareness instead of shame. I honor the strength it took to get here. I respect the work it took to unlearn what no longer served me.

What didn't break me taught me how to live with intention. It taught me how to choose peace even when chaos feels familiar. It trained me how to rebuild trust in myself, and perhaps most importantly, it taught me that wholeness is not the absence of scars. It is the presence of understanding and self-love.

You are not broken. You are learning, growing and mending those holes left by life. Everything you have survived is still teaching you how to become who you were always meant to be.

Six

Fake it Until You Feel it

We have all heard the phrase, "Fake it until you make it," but I have further expanded on the meaning of that since I have learned the importance of feeling. Now, I choose to say, "Fake it until you *feel* it." Once we begin utilizing personal development tools like imagination, creative visualization and affirmations, we realize that sometimes when we buckle down to begin the process we aren't always in the best mood. We may be preparing to say the affirmation: "I am happy and healthy, I am happy and healthy," but at that very moment we don't feel happy or healthy. My suggestion is to go stand in front of a mirror and repeat it anyway. Fake the feeling, pretend as children do. As you continue to speak this powerful affirmation to yourself in the mirror repeatedly, you will eventually begin to actually feel that way. The consistent affirmative stance will transform the negative feeling into a positive one. Positivity wins every time.

I realize many of us are quite busy with our lives and do not feel we have time for long drawn out positive affirmation sessions. That is why I created the #In59seconds Movement. A simple 59 seconds each day of positivity can and will change our lives. While you're running around getting dressed to begin your day. Take 59 seconds to speak to the universe. Speak the perfect day you desire into existence. Tell yourself, "I feel great today,Today is beautiful. Today is a happy day. Today I will make a lot of money. Today everyone will be happy to see me." It does not have to consume a lot of your time. Just 59 seconds of uplifting fuel will do the trick. It can be the very boost you need to ensure a productive day. Use that same 59 seconds to encourage others. Tell your children they are amazing and they have the ability to accomplish anything. Tell your spouse how much you appreciate them and how attractive they look today. This small amount of time of positive empowerment can make a difference in your life and the lives of others. The #In59Seconds Movement can motivate the world.

Words are energy and it has been my experience that repeatedly saying an affirmation aloud will eventually invoke the feeling, and the feeling is the last puzzle piece. Just try it, you have absolutely nothing to lose. Once we couple the positive words with the feelings, that is when the magic of manifestation happens. We must combine the consistent speaking of the words with the feeling of actually having what we desire. This is the perfect recipe to create a great life for yourself.

Many unfortunate situations can and will happen in life. When we allow ourselves to feel bad, we lower our energetic vibration. Despite how justified we are in negatively reacting to a bad situation. We still cannot allow ourselves to stay in the negative state of mind. Thinking negatively lowers our energetic vibration. If we are vibrating at a low frequency then we will attract all things that are also vibrating at that low level. That is why it is vital to learn to raise our vibration as soon as we wake up in the morning. We can raise our own vibration and it's imperative that we do so before we leave the house.

Gospel music is a tool I use daily to feel better. Quite often when I wake up in the morning, my mind is instantly flooded with what bills are due, who I'm upset with, who has disappointed me, what responsibilities I have for the day. Yes, It can be overwhelming. But it's crucial that we do not allow those feelings to continue. We can choose to change how we perceive things. Yes, bills and other financial responsibilities exist however we do not have to perceive them as problems. I now train myself to start thanking God that I have a home to pay a mortgage on rather than being annoyed that the mortgage is due. Instead of agonizing over paying my monthly car note, I remind myself that many don't have vehicles and I continuously put my mind in a state of gratitude that It has always been blessed to have a nice one.

We were born with the natural ability to feel good. We produce natural serotonin in our brains. Serotonin is a chemical messenger that is believed to act as a mood stabilizer. It helps us sleep better. Studies show that high serotonin levels are linked to feeling good and living longer, which should be an ultimate goal for us all.

There are certain foods that increase our body's production of serotonin. Specialists in this field encourage people to eat these specific foods that have been proven to raise the level of serotonin in our bodies. According to the expert these foods include eggs, cheese, pineapples, tofu, salmon, nuts and seeds, and turkey. It may be beneficial to study these foods and others that stimulate serotonin production and choose which of these foods fit best into your daily lifestyle.

When our serotonin levels are low, we may feel irritable, anxious, depressed, pessimistic and experience irregular sleeping patterns. On the contrary, when our serotonin levels are high, we feel happy, energized, and hopeful. Doesn't everyone want to feel happy?

Natural ways to increase serotonin include exercise, cold showers, natural sunshine, prayer, meditation, singing, dancing, and speaking positive affir-mations. There isn't just one way. Find what tools work for you and what compliments your lifestyle and practice it daily. Do not view this practice as a chore. Allow yourself to view participating in these daily practices as you willfully doing something daily to enhance the quality of your life. Even when you simply don't feel it, fake it! Do it anyway. You would be surprised how quickly your feelings will turn around.

I love working out, but sometimes I am lazy, and I simply do not want to do it. I find that if I force myself to get up anyway, shortly after beginning I start to feel so good about myself. Instantly I'll start to see that I have elevated my mood or raised my vibration by pushing myself to do it anyway. Raising one's vibration simply means choosing to operate at a higher frequency. Being happy versus sad, energetic versus a lack of energy, being hopeful versus choosing to focus on all your problems.

The concept of *"fake it until you feel it"* in no way means be unauthentic. It plainly means act as if you feel good until you do. Act as if you want to work out and eventually you will be so grateful that you did. Act as if you have abundance in your life and one day you will. Choose to act pleasant in public as opposed to acting grumpy. Get up and go out into the world and act happy and shortly you will forget that you weren't. Most importantly, you will attract others who are attempting to be positive as well.

When we are parents it is vital that we don't bombard our children with negative phrases like, "This is a horrible day," or "Life sucks." They are listening to our every word. Whether we like or not, they are mentally recording the things they hear us say. To me, this is more of a reason to "fake it". Your five-year-old need not hear the doom and gloom of your life. We owe them a fair chance at happiness, and if all they hear from us is a negative picture of the world, they will begin to feel that way themselves, which is grossly unfair to a child. Show them love and smiles, days filled with happiness and joy and they will grow into happy adults.

There is always something to be grateful for, and expressing that gratitude usually makes you feel better. Let gratitude change your attitude, and in doing so you will learn to drop all those negative labels you put on yourself, and soon you will find yourself becoming a cheerful, motivated, and happy person whom others want to be around.

When I first began speaking motivationally, I had absolutely no experience whatsoever. Other than the few speeches I had given in my Toastmasters International Club, I was a complete novice. Despite being a complete beginner, I started branding myself as a successful motivational speaker. I began dressing the part. I had a professional photo shoot done. I dressed like a speaker. When I walked into a room that I was to deliver a speech in, I was always super nervous. My heart felt like it was going to jump out of my chest each time, yet I walked in the room with confidence. I faked it until I felt it. People would compliment me and give me feedback and called me a seasoned speaker, but I was far from it. Eventually I became that talented, well-seasoned speaker that I pretended to be. I faked it until

I was it. In my mind's eye, I saw myself on stage speaking to huge crowds. I studied other great speakers. I hired several speaking coaches. I attended every speaking seminar I could find. Each year I would travel to attend the Toastmaster International World Championship of Public Speaking. I wanted to surround myself with other people who were doing exactly what I chose to do with the rest of my life. I ordered professional business cards with the words, "Motivational Speaker" in large letters across top of each card. I passed them out to everyone I came in contact with. I didn't introduce myself as SaBrina Fisher Reece, an "aspiring motivational speaker." I proudly greeted them saying "My name is SaBrina Fisher Reece, I am a motivational speaker." Believe in the unseen, act as if you already are exactly who you want to be. Fake it until you feel it and it will become a reality.

Throughout my journey of transformation if ever there was a time that I became discouraged and I was entertaining negative thoughts, I would pick up a book or watch a video by one of our legendary thought leaders. I have read so many books that date as far back as the very early 1900's. Some of my favorite influencers that seem to think very similar to me are: William Walker Atkinson, Eckhart Tolle, Don Miguel Ruiz, Norman Vincent Peale, Greg Braden, Earnest Holmes, Earl Nightingale, Zig Ziglar, W. Clement Stone, Marianne Williamson, Edgar Casey, Joseph Murphy, Nevelle Goodard, Ralph Waldo Emerson, Frederick J. Eikerenkoetter II (Rev. Ike), Joseph Murphy, Robert Collier, and many more. I trained myself to engulf myself in positive thinking whenever I would find myself returning to an old way of thinking. Doing this truly helps it to become a habitual practice. It can take years to retrain our brains and undo all of the negative programming we have lived with most of our lives, but it's vital that we all do it if we sincerely want to have a happy productive life.

The Will

There is something in each of us called, "The Will." The Will is that powerful driving force within us all that gives us the strength and determination to go after what we want. At times it may appear that others have a stronger will than we do. However, we can crank that inner knob on our own "Will" and turn it up to full speed at any point. William Walker Atkinson says, "The Will is the outward manifestation of the 'I Am.'" I completely agree. "I Am" is the most powerful phrase we can say. It leaves no room for future hope and wishes. The statement "I Am," represents now! It represents being completely in the current moment, not believing in or waiting for something to happen later but accepting it as already existing now. Understand the difference between being hopeful for something we desire in the future and claiming that thing to already exist in the present. Even if you can't see or touch it yet, fake it! Feel it! Express gratitude for it now. Act as if it is already there. If you are sad, act happy. If you are poor, act rich. Fake it until you actually feel it and it will soon materialize.

Many people have survived devastating circumstances because they had the will to live. We don't have to wait for a life or death situation to invoke our will. We are the fuel that powers up the Will. When we decide to go full force after our dreams, we find that we are stronger, smarter, and more driven than we could have ever imagined.

As you sit with what you have just read, I invite you to turn some of this attention back toward yourself. Not to judge your past, not to relive it, but to honor what it has shaped in you. Every experience you survived carried information. Every moment you endured taught you something about your strength, your needs, and your capacity to heal. What didn't break you is still speaking, still guiding, still offering wisdom if you are willing to listen. Allow yourself the grace to learn from your life instead of fighting it. Healing does not ask you to forget who you were. It asks you to gently integrate who you have been into who you are becoming.

Seven

Reclaiming the Mind: Closing the Holes from the Inside

One of the most powerful tools I have ever learned during my healing journey is quite simple. It does not require special equipment, money, or permission from anyone else. It begins with awareness. The ability to notice a thought as it enters the mind and make a conscious decision about whether it belongs there.

For years, I did not realize how automatic my thinking had become. Thoughts would enter my mind unchecked, and I accepted them as truth simply because they appeared. I did not question where they came from or whether they were rooted in reality or old pain. I just assumed that whatever my mind presented must be accurate. That assumption quietly kept many of my wounds open.

We cannot change a negative thinking pattern until we first recognize that it exists. That recognition requires stillness. It requires slowing down enough to listen to what is actually happening inside your own mind. Most of us are moving so quickly through life that we rarely pause long enough to hear our internal dialogue. We rush from responsibility to responsibility, managing external demands while ignoring the inner environment that shapes how we experience everything else.

Recognizing that you are actively participating in negative thinking is not an indictment of your character. It is an act of empowerment. Awareness is half the work. Many people spend years suffering without realizing that a significant portion of their daily thoughts are fear-based, self-critical, or rooted in past trauma. When those thoughts go unexamined, they quietly reinforce the very wounds we are trying to heal.

The mind plays a critical role in the quality of life we live. Every experience we have is filtered through thought. Every emotional response is influenced by interpretation. When the mind is dominated by unresolved pain, it continues to reopen old wounds, creating holes that never fully close. Healing requires us to interrupt that cycle.

I often say that the mind is where everything begins. Before anything manifests in the physical world, it exists as a thought. The same is true for emotional realities. Feelings are not visible, but they are powerful. You cannot see sadness or joy floating through the air, yet you can feel their presence deeply. Our actions reveal what is happening inside us long before we speak about it.

Because thoughts hold so much influence, learning to monitor them is essential. I encourage you to think of your mind as a garden. Whatever you plant there will grow. If you consistently plant thoughts of fear, inadequacy, scarcity, or despair, those ideas will take root. Over time, they shape how you see yourself and what you believe is possible. This is how emotional wounds deepen without us even realizing it.

At first, the idea of consciously managing your thoughts may feel overwhelming. Especially if negative thinking has been your default for years. But habits are formed through repetition, and this is a habit worth developing. With practice, awareness becomes easier. Discernment becomes sharper. You begin to notice when a thought does not align with truth, peace, or self-respect.

This awareness is where mending begins.

When I started this work, I created a simple internal practice that helped me regain control of my mind. It began with recognition. I had to slow down enough to notice what I was thinking and how those thoughts made me feel. I learned to distinguish between thoughts that supported my healing and thoughts that reopened my wounds. This was not about labeling myself as negative or positive. It was about understanding what nurtured me and what harmed me.

Once I became aware of a harmful thought pattern, I realized something revolutionary. I did not have to accept every thought that entered my mind. I had the ability to reject it. I call it my "Catch and Cast" system. I catch the negative thought out as soon as it comes in. I stop it in it's tracks, and I cast it out of my mind. That practice alone changed the trajectory of my healing. Many people live their entire lives without knowing they have this choice. They assume thoughts are facts. They are not.

How a thought makes you feel is often the first clue. Does it create fear, shame, guilt, or despair? If so, it deserves examination. Allowing those thoughts to linger is like leaving an open wound untreated. Over time, it becomes infected. Rejection is not suppression. It is discernment. It is choosing not to allow pain-driven thoughts to take up permanent residence in your mind.

Once space is created, replacement becomes possible. This is where healing gains momentum. After removing damaging thoughts, you have room to consciously introduce thoughts that make you feel good. Thoughts that support growth, courage, and self-worth. This is not pretending life is perfect. It is choosing not to relive trauma repeatedly through you mind.

This practice changed my life, but I learned an important lesson along the way. When you are early in healing, vulnerability is heightened. The desire to feel better can make you susceptible to people who promise quick transformation. I learned this the hard way.

During one season of my life, my desperation to heal made me place my power in someone else's hands. I believed another human being could do for me what I had not yet learned to do for myself. I mistook charisma and confidence for wisdom. I mistook spiritual language for spiritual integrity.

That experience taught me something invaluable. No one outside of you holds the key to your healing. Guidance can be helpful, but surrendering your authority is dangerous. Healing is an inside job.

When you have experienced abandonment early in life, you can spend years looking for someone else to fill that void. Sometimes that search shows up in romantic relationships. Sometimes it appears in spiritual spaces. Sometimes it hides in family dynamics. Without awareness, we unknowingly give others power over our sense of worth.

I eventually learned that God had already placed everything I needed inside of me. The tools were always there. I just had to stop outsourcing my healing and start trusting myself.

This realization did not arrive without pain. But it closed a significant hole in my heart. It taught me that while others may walk beside us, the work itself belongs to us alone.

As I continued to turn inward and take responsibility for my healing, I began to understand something that was both humbling and empowering. My deepest wounds did not come only from what had happened to me. They also came from where I placed my power afterward. When you have not received the love you needed at the beginning of life, you can spend years searching for it outside of yourself, believing someone else will finally make things feel whole. That search can quietly keep the holes open.

I saw this pattern show up in my family relationships as well. One of the most complex dynamics in my life was the relationship I had with my sister. It was rooted in love, but it was also shaped by loss, responsibility, and unspoken expectations. Because we grew up without parents in our lives, the roles between us were never simple. She became a protector, a guide, and in many ways, a parental figure, even though she never asked for that responsibility. I leaned into that role without realizing the emotional cost it carried for both of us.

In my brokenness, I placed her on a pedestal that no human being could remain standing on. I looked to her for validation, reassurance, and approval because I had not yet learned how to give those things to myself. I believed that if she was proud of me, then I was safe. If she was disappointed, then I had failed. That dynamic created an imbalance that made it difficult for us to simply be sisters.

At the time, I did not recognize how deeply this affected me and her. I mistook criticism for care and control for protection. When my shortcomings were pointed out, I internalized them as proof that I was not good enough. I did not yet have the emotional strength to say that I was proud of myself, even when I was still learning. I thought love had to be earned through perfection.

What I learned later is that unmet needs do not disappear. They attach themselves to relationships and expectations. When those needs are not fulfilled, the disappointment feels devastating, even when no harm was intended. Understanding this helped me release years of resentment and confusion. It allowed me to see the situation clearly. My sister processed our shared trauma differently than I did. Her strength looked different than mine. Neither of us was wrong. We were both surviving. This awareness helped me mend another hole.

I began to understand that sometimes the people who hurt us do not know they are doing it. Their intent is not always malicious, I am sure my sisters was not. She loved me the best way she knew how. People may truly believe they are helping, guiding, or protecting us. But unresolved pain has a way of transferring itself quietly, even through love. When someone has not examined their own wounds, those wounds can shape how they relate to others. That does not excuse harm, but it does explain it.

Forgiveness became possible when I separated intent from impact. I learned that I could acknowledge how something affected me without assigning blame. That distinction was freeing. It allowed me to heal without hardening my heart.

This understanding also made me reflect on my role as a parent. For years, I kept my children very close. I believed that sheltering them would keep them safe. In reality, I was parenting from fear. I was trying to protect them from the world because I had not yet healed my own relationship with it. My intentions were loving, but my actions were shaped by trauma.

Only after doing my own emotional work could I see how fear had influenced my decisions. What I thought was protection sometimes landed as restriction. This realization required humility. It required me to forgive myself and make space for growth. Healing is not about getting everything right the first time. It is about being willing to adjust when awareness expands.

One of the most important lessons this season taught me is that self-worth cannot be outsourced. No one else can validate you into wholeness. No relationship, teacher, or family member can fill a void that only self-awareness and self-love can address. When we give others control over our emotional health, we place our healing in unstable hands. True happiness begins when we reclaim that power.

I often say that life is like a coloring book, and only you have the crayons. For a long time, I handed my crayons to other people. I allowed their opinions, reactions, and expectations to shape my sense of worth. I let their approval determine my value. Healing required me to take my crayons back and decide what kind of life I wanted to create.

This was not an overnight process. It was gradual and intentional. I had to learn how to recognize the thoughts that reinforced old wounds. I had to reject the internal narratives that told me I was unwanted or unworthy. I had to replace those thoughts with ones rooted in truth. That practice changed everything.

I realized that no one had spent years reminding me of my mother's abandonment. I was the one replaying it in my mind. I was the one keeping the wound open through thought. Once I became aware of that, I understood I had a choice. I could continue suffering, or I could begin mending. This is where real power lives.

Many of us did not have ideal parents. Many of us experienced trauma that shaped how we see ourselves. Those facts matter, but they do not define our future. We are all valuable creations of God with purpose, regardless of what we have endured. Healing requires us to stop reliving the past and start participating in the present.

As I integrated these lessons, I felt myself becoming more whole. The holes did not disappear overnight, but they no longer controlled me. I learned to set boundaries without guilt. I learned to forgive without forgetting. I made a choice to have peace without denying reality.

What I want you to understand is this. Healing does not mean life will never hurt again. It means you no longer allow pain to shape your identity. It means you recognize your worth independent of what others give or withhold. You become the steward of your own emotional and spiritual well-being.

If you are reading this and recognizing yourself in any part of this journey, know that you are not weak. You are becoming aware and awareness is the beginning of change. You do not have to be perfect to be worthy. You do not have to be healed to be whole. You only have to be willing.

Your future is still bright, even if past trauma has dimmed the light. Each day offers an opportunity to choose differently. Every moment offers a chance to respond with intention instead of habit. You are capable of more than you realize.

What life has taken from you does not get the final word. What remains inside you is stronger than anything that tried to break you. The holes can be mended. The mind can be reclaimed. You can move forward knowing that nothing you endured has to effect you forever.

Eight

Close Your Eyes and Visualize

Creative visualization has proven to be so beneficial in my life, which is why I want to share this amazing tool with all of you. I have briefly touched on the subject in the previous chapters, but I want to expand further on it here. We have the power to close our eyes and pretend the things we desire actually exist. Pretending that they exist is the secret to actually manifesting them into your life. Children use their imagination to do this all day long. We are born with this natural ability to create things in our mind. Holding thoughts and images in our minds until we feel as if they are real is the key to bringing all the things we want into our lives. The thoughts we focus on are the ones that matter most. We can control our thoughts, which will give us control over our lives.

Russell Simmons' books, *"Super Rich"* and *"Success Through Stillness,"* along with Eckhart Tolle's *"The Power of Now"* were all instrumental in teaching me the importance of sitting still and monitoring my thoughts. *"Super Rich"* in particular left a great impression on me because being the huge business mogul that Russell is, I'm certain many were drawn to the title believing he was giving the world the secrets of how to attain wealth. I remember how intrigued I was to find that the wealth he spoke of in his book was spiritual and emotional wealth, which are vitally important to sustain financial wealth, but Russell Simmons understood, as I do now, that all the money in the universe won't give you peace of mind.

I get excited about the concepts I speak about in my books and I have unshakable faith in them. However there have been many instances in my life where I had to truly work all the tools I believe in, to recenter myself and return to a place of knowing that what I believe in is indeed real. Life has thrown me many "sucker punches," and during these times I had to reevaluate and reaffirm my beliefs.

I became a grandmother for the first time on June 6, 2019. My oldest daughter, Joi, gave birth to a beautiful baby boy, named Raiden Jesse Spears, named after my father, Jesse Paul Fisher who died when I was ten. Although my daughter and I tried our best to arrange things so I would not miss Raiden's birth, the minute I got onto a plane headed to Tampa, Florida for a speakers' training with Delatorro McNeal III called "Crush The Stage," she went into labor. I could not believe it. I was beyond devastated. All of our efforts to ensure that the baby came before or after my trip had failed. I could not believe I was going to miss the birth of my first grandchild. I was absolutely inconsolable on the plane. This was not a moment I would ever get back.

I'm still not sure how I was able to receive the message in flight with my cell phone on airplane mode, but somehow it came through while I was still in the air. I was so hurt that I was going to miss this monumental occasion that I began to cry uncontrollably. I got up from my seat and went to the back where three stewardesses were preparing to serve lunch to the passengers. I walked into the back where they were and I just cried and cried to them, telling them I was not going to be present for the birth of my first grandchild. They were very sweet and understanding. They hugged me and gave me a bottle of wine to calm me and I returned to my seat. I still couldn't stop crying. My distress was so loud and obnoxious that I felt obligated to explain to the man sitting next to me what the problem was. He was kind and he said some comforting words, which I don't remember, and I laid my head on the window and attempted to suffer through the remainder of the flight silently.

Approximately one hour before the plane landed I took out one of my journals and began to write a poem for my new grandson:

Baby Raiden
I have waited for you all week Lil' guy
And as soon as I'm up in the sky
You choose to say "Hi",
I have cried like a baby on this plane
The stewardesses thought I was in physical pain.
I told them I'm missing your birth.
They said, "Don't cry - celebrate his journey to earth."
I told them that this was a special time.
They comforted me and gave me free wine.
Grammie can't wait to meet you.
Your life will be so Amazing!
We all love you so much.
I can't wait to meet you and feel your soft new touch
I'm so sorry I'm on a plane headed to train, in another state.
Trying to make sure that I am Great!
And worthy of the gift of your love.
My precious Grandson, My Lil' Dove.
I will see you soon. I'm filled with Joy.
Welcome to the world Grammie's Baby Boy.

SaBrina Fisher Reece, 6/4/2019

Aside from being absolutely crushed that I missed the birth of my first grandchild, when the plane descended, I felt the most excruciating pain in my ears. I had done a lot of flying over the past four years and never had I experienced anything this uncomfortable. (This was what led to me making an appointment with the ear, nose, and throat specialist, which resulted in the findings mentioned in Chapter 8). The plane landed and I called my daughter from the airport immediately. She was still en route to the hospital to deliver the baby. I sat down inside the airport and she and I cried and cried on the phone like it was the end of the world. We are very close.

I convinced myself that for whatever reason, I was not meant to be there for the delivery. It was the only thought that calmed me. Maybe God didn't feel I would have been able to see her in so much pain. Fortunately, due to modern technology, I was able to view the entire birth via Facetime.

Although I was grateful that I got to see his birth virtually, the stress of the entire situation caused me to be less than prepared for the three-day intensive speakers training that I went to Tampa, Florida to attend. I was distracted, and it took a ton of positive self-talk to get through the training. Each day when I got back to my hotel room, I had to take a moment to close my eyes and visualize myself inside the classroom, speaking confidently on stage. Fortunately, it was a very small class, which made it a lot easier. I learned that at times we may feel we have done all we can to be the best we can, but when we meet others that are better, we realize we need to keep working harder. Our instructor, Delatorro McNeal III, is a world-renowned speaker, and the confidence he exuded onstage was definitely something I wanted for myself. He challenged me in ways that were clearly necessary, but I was intimidated. During my final speech on the third day, he kept stopping me and making me begin again. My ego led me to believe he was picking on me and I began to take it personally. I know better than to take things personally, but in these moments, I could not fight it off. There was a moment where I had a choice: to sit down, get my feelings in check and return to the stage and deliver my speech again, or walk out. Since walking out is not my style and goes against everything I believe in, I sat down and got my nerves together first, then I began to write affirmations on postcards reassuring myself that I could do this.

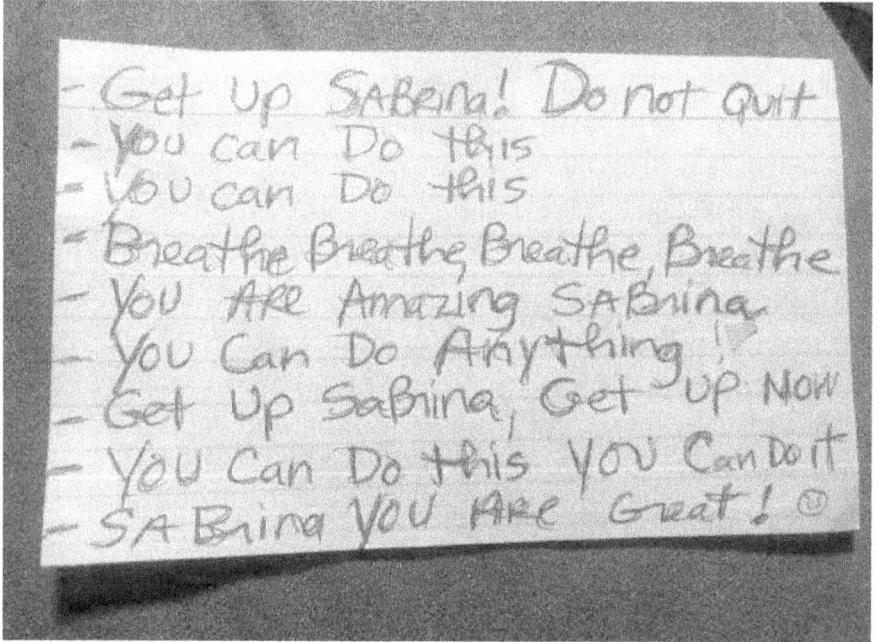

I was scared to death to go back on stage and possibly be stopped mid-speech again, but something inside me knew that if I could get through this, I would be a much better speaker in the end. My heart was pounding. I tried in those few moments to script something, but I knew it was best If I simply spoke from my heart. Other than the instructor and students, several other people had been invited to judge and evaluate our final presentations. That additional pressure definitely didn't make it easier. My old friend, "**Ego**", crept into my mind while I was waiting to go back up again and tried to convince me that the evaluations from the instructor and the guest were biased. "They didn't like me," is what I attempted to tell myself. I wanted to run with that, but one thing I'm excellent at is recognizing ego. Ego is no friend to us and it will distract us from completing tasks we need to evolve to the next level. I traveled to Tampa for this expert training because after years of studying Delatorro McNeal, I knew he was the best, so I quickly told "ego" to shut up and move the heck on, and I continued to breathe and encourage myself.

I got up after restructuring my speech in only fifteen minutes in my head. My nerves were at an all-time high, but mentally I was determined to incorporate some of the techniques that were given to me after my first evaluation. This was one of the hardest things I have ever done. I had to do a lot of self-talk, but I was there to learn. I had to lay my ego down and become completely humble. I felt attacked. I was very emotional and felt like a failure, however it was all in my mind. Not one of the judges called me a failure or said any of those negative things I was thinking to me. I said them to myself in my mind. I had to work through that, and I had to do it quickly. I wanted to scream, walk out, and give up but I knew I would never forgive myself, nor would I learn the lesson that the universe used this moment to teach me. I took several deep breaths and cast away the negative thoughts. I continued my internal affirmations all the way back to the stage.

Needless to say, I did it! I landed it within the allotted ten minutes given to each student. I delivered a magnificent speech, implementing all of the new tools I just learned which earned me my "Crush The Stage" speaking certificate. It helped me advance greatly as a speaker. I learned so much from that experience. I grew in so many areas. I pushed myself when I truly was so emotional from the initial critique that I wanted to give up. I learned to incorporate techniques into my speech that would allow me to humbly sell my book from the stage as well. Selling from the stage is unquestionably something I had no idea how to do. I had been giving my book away because I wanted others to have the skills I used to feel better in life. Most importantly I tested the very tools I teach to others on myself, and they worked! I needed to encourage myself in that uncomfortable moment and I did. Although I thought I was going to die at the time, I am so glad I stuck it out and I would do it all over again.

When I got back to my hotel room to decompress from it all I was so sincerely proud of myself. I utilized the very tools of affirmations and creative visualization to make myself get back on that stage when every ounce of me wanted to quit. I did not quit, and I left there feeling great. Internal work is not always easy, but the mental battles are the very ones we need to win. Going to full-out war with the internal enemies of ego, self-doubt and fear will prove to be the most significant war you will ever fight. I may have missed the birth of my grandson, but I developed something so wonderful with-in myself that made it all worth it. I returned home the next day to meet my beautiful first grandchild.

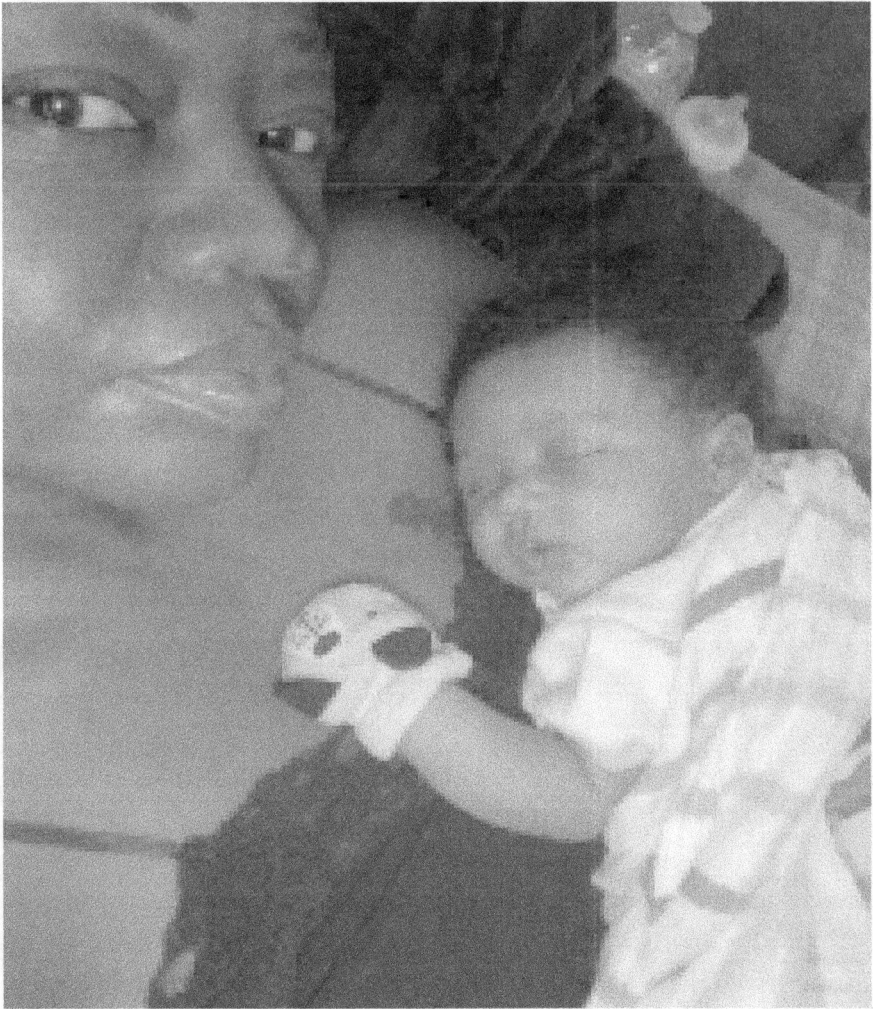

I am so grateful to have lived long enough to see my children's children. There were many times throughout my life that I never thought I would live long enough to see my grandchildren, but once I took control of my life and began to use my natural gift of imagination to create a better life, I became excited about living. I became even more excited about creating a great life. I no longer believe that I was doomed to suffer throughout this life experience as I once did. I began working on changing the narrative in my head. I wanted to live a long healthy life, but I knew I had to mentally create that reality. I had to reprogram all of the images of death. I would practice seeing myself at a much older age. I would create images of having conversations with my great-grandchildren, embracing and encouraging them in full mind, body, and soul. We don't just want to live a long life, we must do the mental work to ensure a long, *healthy* life, free of sickness and disease. No one is meant to simply suffer through life. We are all meant to be happy. Happiness begins inside first. Imagine that you are happy, healthy and prosperous and before you know it you will be.

Training your imagination is not easy, start with simple exercises. Imagine yourself five years from now walking into the home you desire to live in. Imagine the car you want to drive. Imagine the beautiful grass and flowers outside of your new home. If you have a fear of death, imagine yourself at a much later stage in life signifying that you will live a long life. When I get fearful of death, I imagine myself at my eighty-fifth birthday party. I imagine myself smiling and dancing and basking in the joy of being surrounded by all of my children, grandchildren and great-grandchildren. I make sure to be specific in the visual by seeing myself strong and healthy enjoying my birthday. That part is very important. We must be detailed when we do our visualization techniques. You wouldn't want to create a scene where you live to be one hundred but you are sick,disabled, and unhealthy would you? Make sure you visualize yourself happy and healthy. God gave us the power to think anything we desire into existence. This power is active even when we are not aware of it. That is why monitoring our thoughts is necessary.

I have owned several businesses, some of which I knew nothing about before opening. Inked 4 Life Tattoo Studio is proof that you can precisely design something completely in your mind before it exists in the real world. I initially took possession of a commercial building because I created a barber shop for my son Justin who was in barber school. I named that salon, "Just-In-Time Barber and Beauty Salon." After spending an enormous amount of time and money putting this business together it became apparent that my son did not want the responsibility of being a business owner. He said he wanted to become a rapper, which was the dream of so many young African American boys at the time. I always told him that he did not have to continue this as a lifelong career, but it would give him a source of income until he figured out exactly what he wanted to be.

Justin was quite strong-willed, and I was stuck with a barber shop that I had no desire or time to run. I always let my son know that he did not have to make a career out of the barber shop. It was simply my gift to him to generate an income until he was able to pursue his dreams. However he was still quite disinterested in running it. My primary business, Braids By SaBrina, was located two doors down, and it consumed the majority of my time and energy. However, I was locked into a lease for a few years, so I needed to do something with the building. I drove around and scanned the neighborhood for ideas of what I could transform the barber-shop into. I came up with the idea of a tattoo shop. Tattooing was quite popular and there was no direct competitor anywhere near.I knew nothing of how to run this particular type of business. My only experience with tattoo shops was when I had gone to one to receive a tattoo. However, in my mind I began to create the business. This was at a time in my life where I had no idea the importance of creative visualization. I had not yet learned these mental tools, but by default I designed this business in my mind from beginning to end. It had beautiful, fluorescent green lettering to catch the attention of those in oncoming traffic. Fortunately, I was able to utilize most of the furniture from the barber shop. I did a lot of the artwork on the wall myself. I even drew a large koi fish on the floor. It was a fun and exciting new experience.

In my sleep, I would come up with ideas and then get up and implement them the next day. I repeat I had no experience whatsoever in the tattoo industry. I went around town and visited other tattoo parlors to get an idea of the basic setup. Thirty days later I opened the doors to Inked 4 Life Tattoo

Studio on Adams Blvd. A full- fledged business that began as a simple thought.

Our minds are so amazing. The mind is indeed magical. Even before I knew how to use visualization techniques as a tool, I was successful in using them by default. When I think back on how I used my mind to create that business, I get inspired. I never allowed fear or doubt to enter my mind. I never once remember thinking that it was not possible to own a tattoo shop. I visualized it and voila! I became the sole proprietor of yet another successful business. That opportunity exists for everyone. Thinking back on that reminds me that we can do absolutely anything as long as we ignore those little voices in our heads that tell us we cannot.

We are creators and anything we truly desire we can have. I believe this should be taught in kindergarten. Children should learn, as early as possible of the power they possess over their own lives. They should be taught that their lives are like a coloring book and only they possess the crayons. I believe that mankind can indeed evolve, but it starts with each and every individual person recognizing their own greatness. We all must come to terms with the fact that we are not limited unless we choose to be. We can become anyone we chose to become. The possibilities are limitless. We can acquire any level of success we choose. We simply have to train our minds to believe that all things are possible.

Nine

How do I Hold it Together?

All things are possible, and I know it's hard for us to believe that at times, especially when everything in our lives seems to be going wrong and all of what we desire hasn't shown up. Times when that home loan was denied, or our relationship seems to be falling apart. Maybe we have lost our job, or our car has been repossessed. It seems that none of our prayers have been answered. These are the times when it's hardest to believe that all things are possible, but they are.

It is during these times when we feel defeated that we allow our vibration to become low. We are all energy and we are all vibrating. We appear to be solid, as do the chair we sit in or the car we drive, but everything is vibrating. You can't see it, but you are vibrating at this very moment. What most don't know is that they can change the frequency of their personal vibration. We can choose to vibrate at a higher frequency. It seems natural that during the hardest times of our lives, when tragedy strikes us or our families, or when finances are low and no ends seem to meet, that we feel stressed and afraid. Acknowledge those feelings, but don't stay there. No matter what you are going through, you still have to encourage yourself and raise your vibration.

I became inspired once I realized that I could change the way I felt. I never had to accept being in a bad mood, no matter what I believed the cause of it to be. If by chance I woke up feeling down, learning that I did not have to accept those feelings and carry them throughout my day was very helpful. We all have the opportunity to reject negative feelings as soon as we recognize them and use whichever tool we find effective in making ourselves instantly feel better. Gospel music or listening to 432 hz binaural beats works well for me. The gospel music instantly makes me happy and grateful. The pure tone version of the 432 hz binaural beats helps me to concentrate,especially when writing. Find what works for you and don't hesitate to use it center yourself and to uplift your mood.

A quick way for me to pull myself out of a negative space is to write down and acknowledge the things I have to be grateful for. We all have many things to be grateful for. If you are having money problems, but you still have a job, then you have something to be grateful for. If your car isn't running at its best but it's still running and getting you to that job everyday, then you have something to be grateful for. If you are employed, allow yourself to feel gratitude for having a job when many do not. Simply taking a moment to sit with and bask in those feelings of gratitude will instantly encourage you. Feeling encouraged motivates us to accomplish more in life.

It is imperative that we realize it takes a conscious effort to make positive change on a subconscious level. If we want a better, more productive life, especially internally, then we must take external steps towards securing our internal happiness. We must come to understand that the internal is just as important or even more important than the external. We must work daily on the subjective aspect of happiness in order to reap the objective benefits of a great life. Subjective things are things you cannot see, feel or touch. Objective things are tangible, things we can touch and see. If we master subjective/internal happiness, objective/external happiness is soon to follow.

Like attracts like. Positive attracts positive and negative attracts negative. It is an immutable universal law. Just like gravity and karma. No matter what you do or who you are if you jump off the roof of a building you will go down. The results of karma are not as visible, but they are unchangeable as well. Kindness returns unto you kindness, hate returns hate it's unavoidable.

Universal laws are laws that are inflexible and not subject to change. They are the laws of God.

The Law of Attraction is definitely something you should familiarize yourself with. You attract back to you exactly the energy and vibration that you put out into the world. If you get up in the morning and you aren't feeling your best, take a few minutes before you get up to raise your vibration. Intentionally uplift the way you feel inside so the energy you release into the world is positive. Don't allow yourself to stay in a bad mood or stay sad, unhappy, or disappointed. Low energy attracts more low energy. High energy does the same. We can't afford to proceed with the tasks of our day without elevating our energetic frequency. If you want to have a great day, take a few moments and first speak that intent into the universe. Actually, say the words "Today will be a great day." Better yet, say, "Today Is a great day." Speak of it as a fact and not a wish. Repeat that while you brush your teeth and do your other morning rituals. What most people aren't aware of is that words and thoughts have an energetic frequency too. When you speak negatively, saying things such as, "I'm broke," "I'm dumb," or "I will never get ahead in life," you project that negativity into the world. What you send out comes back. Let's work on making sure the things that come back are good and positive.

We are subconsciously programmed to instantly put up barriers to impede our own thoughts of greatness and success. Try to monitor your thoughts enough to catch yourself the next time it happens. Eventually it will become a positive habit that will change your life.

I used to say to myself, "I want to own a laundromat," but no sooner than the thought came into my mind, I would have thoughts which said, "No, that's too much work," or "Where would you find all those washing machines? You know nothing about this type of business SaBrina." These are self-sabotaging thoughts. This is an example of how we talk ourselves out of greatness. These are the barriers I am speaking of. We create these untruths in our minds. It is for us to simply plant the seed in the garden and allow it to grow. Plant a positive seed not a negative one. We need not concern ourselves with the particulars of how it will be manifested, we just need to believe wholeheartedly that it will. We absolutely must "believe in things unseen as if they already are"

"Now Faith is the substance of things hoped for, the evidence of things unseen."
(Hebrew 11:1)

This may not always be the easiest thing to do, but it's the key to being able to manifest your heart's desires into your life. Pretend! Pretend as a child would. Pretend you have that home you want; pretend you have already opened that business you have been dreaming about. Commit an extensive amount of time thinking about it. Literally close your eyes and see the big "Grand Opening" sign in your mind. Design the lettering and the colors. Visualize the people coming in the front door with big smiles congratulating you on the opening day of your business. Force yourself to smile and allow yourself to fill up inside with pride for your accomplishment. Stick with that visual long enough to actually feel the corresponding emotion at that moment. Keep the images in your head until you can connect emotions with them as well. The visual Image plus emotion is key. You'll know it's working when you find yourself smiling externally and internally.

I can always tell when I am following my destined path. People will show up in my life and strike up a conversation that mirrors my own concepts and beliefs. This positive thinking ideology is not always well-received. Many times, I am hesitant to bring up the way I think to others. Even as I type this, I know that despite a huge percentage of the world not being open enough to hear and accept that we are in control of our destiny, and that our thoughts and feelings shape that very destiny, I know that my purpose here on this earth is to continue to deliver that message. Part of my mission here on Earth is to teach people the tools I used to transform my mindset, which ultimately transformed my entire life.

When I come across an author, thought, leader, or speaker who seems to be on the same path I'm on, it makes me emotional. Positive emotions flood through me because even if those people never know I read their book, or watched their videos, my life was impacted by their work because they followed their purpose. My goal is to do the same for others with my literary work. My books and speeches will impact lives. That is what motivates me to continue. The fact that others will learn to love themselves and live their lives to the fullest makes it all worth it.

All things are possible. See yourself in your mind's eye exactly as the person you want to be. You can be anyone you truly want to be. In no way am I insinuating that developing intentional positive pictures in your head is easy. It takes work and a lot of practice. However, this will be the best skill you've ever learned. Mastering this skill will allow you to take part in all the wonderful things this world has to offer.

The practice of creative visualization will get easier and easier. You can hone this skill by attempting to visualize small things like a banana. Close your eyes and tell your mind you see a banana, then switch it to an apple. Learning to creatively visualize takes practice. The images may seem fuzzy or unclear at first. As you continue to do it you will see how quickly the images you call upon appear faster and faster the more you practice this technique. Eventually the images will be clear and solid. You will see how the mind creates pictures instantly as soon as we think of them. That's how God and the universe work. Plant the image with your thoughts and let God do the rest. Remember mastering this ability takes focused intentional time and practice just like any other skill. Please don't get frustrated and quit. Sticking with this will change your life as it did mine. This is the amazing magic of your mind.

We no longer have to live in a world where we have to sacrifice some of our desire for others. Everything is a possibility; we simply have to learn how to bring them to us. We don't have to give up on wealth to have happiness, or sacrifice the desire for peace in order to be successful. We can have it all. These positive practices are how I have held it together over the years.

I don't know anyone who does not want more of something in life, be it peace of mind, abundant wealth, or happiness. Everyone has hopes and dreams of something more. This book will reinforce the fact that you can indeed have exactly what you want and plenty of it. However, many people are unsure of exactly what they desire. What do you want? What will make you happy? Sit down and clarify in detail precisely what you believe needs to be added to your life to make you pleased and content. Our thoughts escape us at times. We will think or dream of something and after proceeding with our daily activities we will forget. I suggest always keeping a journal with you to jot down your thoughts, goals and ideas as quickly as your mind delivers them to you. Many of those ideas will prove to be quite valuable. Later, you can pick one at a time and visualize having it. Give each thing you list in your journal its own individual creative visualization time. Practice this positive tool daily and soon it will astonish you how fast all of the wonderful things show up in your life.

Remember, all things are possible; not some, but all. I repeat that continuously because I want you to know that there is no goal that is too big. *It's all possible!* Accepting that is one of the first steps in changing your life through positive thinking. There are no limits other than the ones we accept in our mind. We must learn how to maintain a positive state of mind, because doing so will drastically change the things that show up in our lives. Remember that the mind is our own personal garden. It accepts exactly what we plant. It's our genie in a bottle. The mind will grant our true wishes, good or bad. We must understand that. The mind won't say, "No, I don't think that is a good idea." If you plant it, it will grow!

Everything you desire is possible, bad things included. We must not focus on bad thoughts. We have the ability to manifest undesirable things into our lives also. Things that are not in our best interest or in line with God's plan for us are also possible. *All* things are possible, so we must guide our thoughts toward the possibilities we sincerely want in our lives.

Do not waste time thinking and fearing that you will have a car accident, or you will. Do not focus your mind power on your fears of divorce or that is the very thing that will happen to your marriage. The thoughts we allow our minds to concentrate on will show up in our actual lives. Many of us do not realize how much time we spend thinking of the things we fear.

What you fear will appear! You can be certain of that. Take time to identify what those fears are so you can recognize them when they show up in your mind and quickly eliminate them.

Once we fully understand that anything we apply focused thought to can and will appear in our lives, then we should not continue to resist the fact that it's necessary to learn to focus on the good and positive, and cast out all other thoughts before they materialize. Many of the things present in my life today, I have to admit, I committed a significant amount of time thinking of them. Good or bad, the rules are the same. Catch yourself the next time you find yourself daydreaming. It may seem harmless, but once you stop yourself and immediately reflect back to what you were just daydreaming about, you may find it was not positive. If that is the case, then you will see why this practice is necessary. Catch those negative, fearful thoughts immediately and switch them into positive ones.

The Bible states in Matthew 19:26, *"But Jesus Beheld them and said unto them, "With men this is impossible, but with God all things are possible"* or in Luke 1:37 *"For with God nothing shall be impossible."* Growing up in the Christian church I have heard many different versions of these scriptures combined with their many different interpretations. I believe that from the beginning of time God created us with no limitations. We have always been capable of great, amazing things but somehow we lost our way. At some point in our existence humans seemed to accept restrictions on our lives that were never meant to exist, restrictions that technically do not exist until we convince ourselves that they do. This has been the downfall of mankind. This is why everyone is not a successful inventor, adding their life-changing contributions to the world. We all are capable of great ideas. We are all great. That amazing inspiration for creation is inside of us all. We just need to remember that it's there.

Watching inspirational movies of people who persevered despite great odds and accomplished their dreams are great reminders that we can do anything. Stories such as that of Bart Millard, the lead singer of the group, Mercy Me, have uplifted me. His life story inspired the world in the movie and hit song, "I Can Only Imagine." I've watched this movie at least a dozen times. The feelings of hope that you feel when you watch others strive for success and win are priceless. This is often the push we need to keep going until we accomplish our goals. Knowing that all of our goals are attainable should keep that fire burning in all of us.

Another story that inspired me was the story of Tommy Caldwell and Kevin Jorgeson. They were rock climbers determined to conquer a massive mountain in El Capitan called, "The Dawn Wall." When I began watching the documentary my first thought was, *Why would anyone want to do this?* Once I finished the show, I realized it does not matter if others understand the "why" as long as we do. Whatever stirs up that drive and gives us the will power needed to recognize that we can do anything is all that matters. For some, it may be climbing the highest mountain. For others, it may be running for president or becoming a best-selling author. Many may have dreams of acting on the big screen or becoming a great singer. Whatever it is that motivates us as humans to keep going, that is what we all need to hold on to.

All goals are attainable. There is no goal you can set for yourself that is too big to accomplish. Do not allow anyone to convince you of that. More importantly, do not convince yourself that certain goals are unattainable. Nothing you desire is insurmountable. If you are willing to commit to the work needed to bring your desires into your reality, then nothing can stop you from achieving them. Yes, the physical work, the hustle and bustle are important, but the most important work is the mental work; learning to keep your thoughts positive. Believe that what you want is already done, not "will be," not "one day," but already done. Close your eyes and feel the feelings of already having what you desire. And like magic you will reap the objective benefits of having it. There is nothing that is impossible. Get a pen and paper, write down your clearly defined goals and get to work.

I am aware that it is a whole lot harder to hold it together when you are struggling financially. This is one concept that made it easier for me. Abundance is a concept that I speak about regularly. I have several Youtube videos entitled. "**Abundance Is Real** by SaBrina Fisher Reece." I am very passionate about the fact that I believe all people can experience abundance in all areas of their lives. Financial abundance is something people feel that they have to sacrifice in exchange for good health, happiness, and peace. We do not have to forgo wealth. We can have financial abundance too.

Yes, working hard is half the battle, but I am of the mindset that prosperity begins first in the mind. **Your Mind is Magic,** and our minds are the magic wand that will allow financial wealth to show up in our lives. The action of work is secondary. One can work all day and night but if he doesn't believe that he deserves abundance he won't have it.

There is a scripture in the bible that says, *"For whoever has, he shall be given more, and they will have abundance. Whoever does not have, even what they have will be taken from them".* Matthew 13:12

I think many people misinterpret this scripture as God being cruel. That's not it at all. Since poverty is a mindset, God is simply saying for those who believe they deserve wealth will receive more, but for those who gain some degree of financial freedom, but are still of the mindset that they don't deserve it, they will eventually lose it. They will lose it not because they don't deserve it, but because they don't believe that they deserve it. They are surprised by the prosperity, so they expect to lose it. We must train our minds to expect wealth.

Have you ever noticed how some big business tycoons lose everything and go bankrupt, yet somehow rebuild everything in a short amount of time? The only thing they possess that differs from many others is the expectation of success. They see themselves as nothing but wealthy even when their business has failed. Poverty is a mindset that can be changed. No one has to settle for poverty. The first steps in changing it begins in the mind.

Each one of us is entitled to the riches of the world, but we cannot experience that wealth in its entirety until we rid our minds of a poverty mindset. Understandably, after years of expecting financial hardship it can take a lot of consistent work to reverse those habits. Begin with a simple daily affirmation:

"I am rich in all areas of my life, money flows frequently
and effortlessly into my life."

Abundance is real and something we all can enjoy. Make a decision that no matter what your current financial situation, you will begin to thank God daily for abundance. Even if your mind is trying to convince you that you are being dishonest, keep putting thoughts of gratitude out into the universe. Keep telling God, "Thank you," for the wealth he has blessed you with. Act as if you are the wealthiest person in the world. Mentally declare prosperity for yourself and believe me it will appear. Do not try to concern yourself with how and where it will come from. Just believe that is possible and that it is already done.

Ten

Mending the Mind: Where Healing Truly Begins

Positive thinking is just as essential to our lives as food is to our bodies. Just as we need daily nourishment to survive physically, we need intentional, healthy thought patterns to survive emotionally and spiritually. They aid in the mending of our holes. Without them, life can begin to feel heavy, dark, and limited. When the mind is left unattended, it often defaults to fear, lack, and hopelessness. That is not because we are weak, but because pain has a way of hijacking our inner dialogue.

People who struggle to think positively often feel powerless. They believe life is something that happens to them, not something they participate in shaping. They assume they must accept whatever circumstances come their way, even when those circumstances are rooted in past trauma or early wounds. That belief alone can deepen the holes life has already created in the heart. But that belief is not the truth. Mending the mind is a first step in mending those holes let behind by life.

While it is true that many of us experienced situations in childhood that were completely out of our control, adulthood offers something different. It gives u a choice. It offers the opportunity to reclaim authority over the mind.

Once you learn how to recognize and manage your thinking patterns, you no longer have to suffer endlessly from what has already happened to you. You no longer have to relive old trauma on repeat. You can interrupt those cycles and create new positive memories. You can intentionally create moments of peace, joy, and gratitude even while healing is still in progress.

This is where the mending begins. This is precisely why I wrote *Unbroken*. Not because life has been easy for me, but because it has not. I needed to learn that this world is not inherently cruel, even though cruel things happen within it. Painful experiences do not cancel out the possibility of happiness. Trauma does not disqualify us from joy. We can all be happy, healthy and healed. Healing does not require us to deny what hurt us. It requires us to decide how much power we will continue to give it.

When I was younger, I never believed that happiness was available to me. I truly thought I had suffered too much. I believed sadness was my destiny and that depression was simply the price I would pay for surviving what I had survived. That belief shaped my reality for many years. But it was wrong.

What changed my life was not luck or circumstance. It was application. It was me deciding that enough was enough and getting up and taking charge of my own healing process. I began using the very tools I now share with you. Slowly, intentionally, and imperfectly, I retrained my mind. Over time, my life transformed in ways I never could have imagined. I went from being a hopeless and suicidal young woman to becoming a business owner, a sound meditation teacher, an author, a spiritual artist, and a motivational speaker. None of that happened because I was special. It happened because I was willing to do the internal work.

Those opportunities are not exclusive to me. They exist for everyone. You can also decided to gain control of the thoughts that do not serve you. No matter what you have been through, what you have lost, or what holes life has left in your heart, possibility still exists. But healing always begins in the same place. The mind. You must get your mind aligned before your life can follow.

I often say, "Mind is all." That phrase has stayed with me for years, and it remains one of the foundational truths of my work. Everything that exists in the physical world began as a thought. The device you are reading this on was once an idea in someone's mind. The buildings we live in, the systems we navigate, the art we admire, all of it originated in thought first.

Emotions work the same way. Feelings are mental experiences. You cannot physically see sadness or happiness. There is no visible cloud of joy that floats around happy people. Emotions are unseen, yet incredibly powerful. What we do see are the actions that follow those emotions. The mind interprets experiences, assigns meaning to them, and then tells the body how to respond.

Fear, inadequacy, self-doubt, and hopelessness are all products of the mind. That does not make them imaginary or invalid, but it does mean they can be challenged. Since the mind influences so much of our experience, learning to take authority over it is one of the most powerful forms of self-healing available to us.

This book is not asking you to pretend everything is fine. When I use the word positive, I am not advocating for denial, perfection, or toxic optimism. I am not suggesting that you ignore pain or bypass grief. I am reminding you that you are a perfect creation of God, even with your flaws, even with your scars, even with the holes life has left behind.

Perfection, in this sense, is not about flawlessness. It is about wholeness. It is about recognizing your worth without requiring yourself to be fixed first. When you accept and love yourself as you are, you create space for healing to occur naturally. You begin mending the holes from the inside out.

The goal is not to force positivity. The goal is to choose the more favorable option whenever possible. To pause before reacting. To consider another perspective. To give yourself the benefit of compassion instead of criticism.

When anger rises, and it will, the invitation is to stop. To breathe. To think before responding. A single pause can change the entire outcome of a situation. A moment of awareness can prevent words that cannot be taken back. Anger is understandable, but it is rarely productive. It is a low-vibrational response that often creates more damage than resolution.

When you respond from anger and hurt, you tend to invite more of it. But when you choose patience, love, and kindness, even when it feels difficult, you raise the emotional frequency of the moment. You create safety where there was once tension. You begin mending wounds instead of ripping them open.

This is not easy work. Healing never is. But it is worthy work. Every time you choose awareness over reaction, you stitch another thread into the places life once tore open. Every time you challenge a negative thought, you reclaim a piece of yourself that was lost to fear. Every time you pause and choose love, you reinforce the truth that you are not broken. You are healing.

The mind may not be where the holes began, but is the key location to where they are mended. That is why *Unbroken* exists. Not to tell you that life will never hurt again, but to remind you that you are capable of healing, choosing differently, and creating a life that reflects peace instead of pain. The storm may have shaped you, but it does not get to define you.

You are still here. You are still great, and you are still unbroken.

About the Author

SaBrina Fisher Reece understands what it means to keep going without applause.

For over twenty-six years, she built one of the most influential braiding salons and schools in Los Angeles-**Braids By SaBrina**-earning recognition throughout California as "The Braid Queen." Her name was on the door, her reputation on the line, and her success was self-made. But behind the achievements was a quieter truth: much of her journey was navigated without consistent support, validation, or encouragement from others.

SaBrina's life has been shaped by early abandonment, profound loss, and hard-earned self-trust. Those experiences taught her that confidence on the outside does not always mean peace on the inside, and that real strength is learned when you are forced to become your own support system.

Today, SaBrina is an author, speaker, and guide focused on emotional growth, self-mastery, and inner alignment. She is the author of several transformational works, including *My Spiritual Smile: Tools for Mental and Emotional Transformation*, ***Your Mind Is Magic***, ***Perfectly Positive:*** *How to Stay Positive when Life is Not Perfect*, ***Spiritual Balance:*** *Aligning Mind, body* *and Energy in Everyday Life,* **Living Life on a Higher Frequency:** *Daily Steps to Raising your Personal Vibration,* **How to Get Exactly What You Want From God:** *Mastering the Art of Effective Prayer,* **Kicking Depression in the Butt:** *How to Battle the Internal Enemy and Win,* **Self Sabotage:** *Learning not to be your own worst enemy,* **Become Your own Cheerleader:** *Moving Forward in Life Without the Support of Others,* **Family Fun Night Cookbook, When I Say 'I Am", and How to Make More Money in 2026,** Over 50 and Still Fine- Lookin got Date Again. Each reflects a chapter of her own evolution.

Now residing in New Mexico, SaBrina continues her work through writing, sound-based healing practices and helping others bring their literary dreams to print through **In59Seconds Publishing Co.** She is always reminding readers that there is no single path to peace, only the courage to walk your own.

Her message is simple and unwavering:

Sometimes the most important applause you will ever receive is the one you give yourself.

You can connect with me on:

🌐 https://in59secondspublishing.com

f https://www.facebook.com/BraidQueenSaBrinaReece

Also by SaBrina Fisher Reece

For more than twenty-six years, she built one of the most influential braiding salons and schools in Los Angeles, **Braids By SaBrina**, earning statewide recognition as *"The Braid Queen."* Her success was self-made, built through discipline, resilience, and vision, often without consistent support or validation from others.

Shaped by early abandonment, profound loss, and hard-earned self-trust, SaBrina's life journey led her to explore emotional healing, spiritual alignment, and self-mastery. Today, she is an author, speaker, and guide dedicated to helping others develop inner balance, confidence, and emotional strength.

She is the author of numerous self-help and transformational works, including *My Spiritual Smile, Your Mind Is Magic, Perfectly Positive, Spiritual Balance, Living Life on a Higher Frequency, Become Your Own Cheerleader, Kicking Depression in the Butt, Self Sabotage, How to Get Exactly What You Want From God,* *When I Say

Spiritual Balance

Spiritual Balance: Aligning Mind, Body, and Energy in Everyday Life is a grounded, insightful guide for anyone seeking clarity, emotional stability, and deeper alignment in a fast-moving world.

In this book, SaBrina Fisher Reece explores the truth that many people sense but struggle to articulate: life becomes chaotic when our inner energies are out of balance. Drawing from spiritual principles, lived experience, and practical awareness, *Spiritual Balance* breaks down how the mind, body, and energetic self are deeply interconnected—and how neglecting one inevitably affects the others.

This book reframes common spiritual concepts in a way that is accessible, realistic, and applicable to everyday life. Readers will learn that masculine and feminine energies are not tied to gender, but are universal forces present within every person. When these energies are balanced, we experience greater peace, confidence, emotional regulation, and healthier relationships. When they are not, stress, confusion, and emotional exhaustion take over.

Rather than offering abstract philosophy, *Spiritual Balance* provides readers with a new way of understanding themselves. It encourages self-awareness, intentional living, and emotional responsibility without shame or perfectionism. Topics include emotional balance, energetic boundaries, spiritual awareness, self-worth, and the role of unseen forces in shaping our daily experiences.

This book is for readers who know there is more to life than what can be seen, measured, or explained logically—but who also want something practical, grounded, and honest. *Spiritual Balance* meets spirituality where real life happens: in relationships, work, healing, growth, and everyday decisions.

By aligning mind, body, and energy, readers are guided toward a more peaceful, empowered, and intentional way of living—one that honors both the human experience and the spiritual truth beneath it.

PROFOUND
Introduction to the Profound Series

This series was not written to convince you of anything.

It was written to remind you of something.

For most of my life, I searched for answers the same way many people do. I looked outward. I prayed, studied, worked, endured, and tried to become better by force. I believed growth meant effort alone and that transformation required suffering. I was taught, as many of us are, what to believe, what to question, and what to avoid.

What I did not realize at the time was that I was not missing faith.

I was missing understanding.

The *Profound Series* was born from a deeply personal journey of self-discovery, healing, and expansion. It is the result of decades of reading ancient texts, studying metaphysical teachings, reflecting on spiritual principles, and most importantly, applying this wisdom in real life. This series is not meant to replace religion, tradition, or belief systems. It is meant to widen the lens.

Religion offers structure, community, and devotion. Ancient wisdom offers context, depth, and responsibility. Together, they reveal something powerful: that you are not separate from the divine, and you were never meant to live disconnected from your inner power.

This series exists because I discovered that much of what we are seeking has already been known for centuries. Long before modern psychology, neuroscience, or self-help, ancient philosophers, mystics, teachers, and spiritual scholars understood the relationship between thought, emotion, consciousness, and reality. They understood that the mind is creative, that belief shapes experience, and that life responds to awareness.

The first book, **Profound**, is about remembering. It is about gathering ancient wisdom and recognizing truths that may feel familiar even if you are encountering them for the first time. This is the awakening stage. The moment when something inside you says, "There is more."

The second book, **Activate**, is about embodiment. Knowledge alone does not change a life. It must be practiced. This book moves wisdom from the intellect into daily living. It teaches you how to tap into the divine energy within you and apply what you have learned in practical, grounded ways.

The third book, **Think**, is about mastery of the mind. Thought is not passive. It is creative. This book guides you in becoming aware of your inner dialogue, understanding how thoughts shape experience, and learning how to consciously direct the mental patterns that influence your life.

The fourth book, **Live**, is about integration. This is where knowledge, practice, and awareness become who you are. You no longer strive to be aligned. You live aligned. You move through the world with clarity, compassion, and confidence, embodying the wisdom you have gained.

Together, these four books form a complete journey.

Awakening. Activation. Mastery. Expression.

This is not a quick fix. It is not spiritual bypassing. It is not about perfection. It is about responsibility. Responsibility for your thoughts. Responsibility for your emotional state. Responsibility for the energy you bring into the world.

The world does not need more information. It needs more conscious people. People who are self-aware. People who understand cause and effect at the level of thought and emotion. People who can pause, reflect, and respond instead of react. People who live from inner alignment rather than fear.

You were never meant to live small, disconnected, or powerless. You were meant to participate in your own evolution.

This series is an invitation. Not to abandon what you believe, but to expand it. Not to follow me, but to follow your own inner knowing. Not to search endlessly outside yourself, but to reconnect with what has always been within you.

If you are reading this, you are ready.

Ready to remember.

Ready to activate.

Ready to master your mind.

Ready to live fully.

Welcome to the journey.

How to Get Exactly What You Want From God

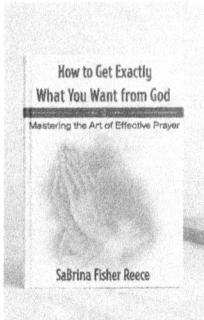

How to Get Exactly What You Want From God: Mastering the Art of Effective prayer: shows you how to pray with results. Inside, you'll learn how to make specific requests, build the faith needed to sustain them, and match your thoughts and emotions to the outcome you want. SaBrina teaches you how to interrupt negative self-talk, eliminate doubt, and step into a mindset that attracts divine answers quickly and clearly. This is your guide to intentional prayer, spiritual alignment, and receiving blessings without hesitation.

What if prayer was never meant to be begging, pleading or waiting in doubt - but instead a powerful alignment with what God has already promised you?

In this amazing book *SaBrina Fisher Reece* dismantles the myths around ineffective prayer and exposes the spiritual authority each believer already possesses. Blending deep spiritual wisdom, real life testimonies of divine intervention, and the practical mindset of a seasoned entrepreneur. SaBrina teaches readers how to pray with confidence, clarity, gratitude and expectation, so they can finally see there hearts desires appear in real time.

Through powerful personal stories of protection, provision, survival and miraculous alignment, SaBrina reveals that prayer becomes effective when belief replaces fear and faith replaces uncertainty. The Kingdom of Heaven is already within you. This book is not about religion as routine - it is about relationship, authority and conscious co-creation with God.

In this book you will learn:
. Eliminate doubt from your prayer
. Speak with spiritual authority and conscious intention
. Align your thoughts, emotions and actions with your prayers
. Recognize Divine intervention in your life
. Trust God's timing without losing hope
This is not a book about hoping and wishing.
This is a book about knowing and trusting that "It Already Done!"
Effective prayer doesn't wonder if God will move - it prepares your

life for when He does

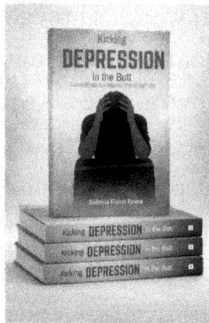

Kicking Depression in the Butt

Kicking Depression in the Butt is a raw, faith-infused, and deeply practical guide for anyone who is tired of surviving in silence and ready to reclaim their life.

Drawing from her own lived experiences with trauma, abandonment, loss, and depression, SaBrina Fisher Reece invites readers into an honest conversation about what depression really feels like, and how to fight back. This book does not minimize pain or offer shallow positivity. Instead, it helps readers recognize depression as an internal enemy, interrupt destructive thought cycles, and rebuild their inner world with intention, truth, and daily tools that actually work.

Through personal storytelling, spiritual insight, and mindset-shifting strategies, SaBrina shows readers how to stop identifying with their darkest thoughts and begin designing a life that protects their peace. She addresses the realities of trauma, triggers, boundaries, faith, therapy, medication, and personal responsibility, offering a balanced approach that honors both professional support and inner work.

Kicking Depression in the Butt is for the person who keeps showing up while quietly falling apart. It is for those who smile while suffering, who feel strong on the outside but exhausted on the inside. Most of all, it is a reminder that depression may visit, but it does not get to stay, and it does not get to become your identity.

This book is not about perfection. It's about progress. It's about learning how to fight for your mind, your peace, and your future, one thought, one choice, and one day at a time.

Because as long as you have breath in your body, your story is not over, and you still have the power to kick depression in the butt.

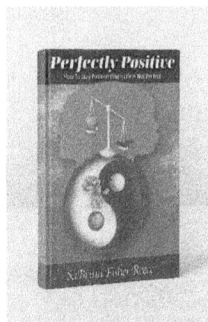

Perfectly Positive

Perfectly Positive is your guide to staying centered, grounded, and hopeful in an imperfect world. Through real-life stories, practical tools, and soul-level wisdom, SaBrina Fisher Reece shows you how to rise above daily stress, disappointments, and negative thinking to create a life rooted in peace and purpose. This book teaches you how to master your thoughts, elevate your vibration, and choose a positive perspective, even when life isn't cooperating. Inspiring, relatable, and deeply transformative, *Perfectly Positive* reminds you that happiness is not found in perfection... it's created by the power of your own mi

Over 50 and Still Fine

Over 50 and Still Fine: Looking to Date Again explores the realities of midlife dating with honesty, humor, and emotional depth. In this reflective and empowering work, author SaBrina Fisher Reece examines the healing process required to re-enter the dating world after loss, long-term relationships, or extended periods of self-focus.

Blending personal experiences with insight and encouragement, the book addresses the emotional challenges, shifting expectations, and renewed self-awareness that often accompany dating later in life. Rather than offering a formula for romance, Reece emphasizes self-worth, emotional clarity, and the importance of honoring one's boundaries while remaining open to connection.

This book speaks to readers seeking authenticity, growth, and laughter as they navigate the evolving landscape of relationships. **Over 50 and Still Fine** affirms that dating at any age can be a meaningful extension of self-discovery, healing, and personal empowerment.

www.ingramcontent.com/pod-product-compliance
Lightning Source LLC
Chambersburg PA
CBHW062018040426
42447CB00010B/2055